NOW I CAN
FLY!

by JANE McWHORTER

QUALITY PUBLICATIONS
P.O. BOX 7385
FT. WORTH, TX 76111
(800) 359-7708

Dedicated to Greg and Kathy
who have brought such pride and pleasure
to their parents

ISBN: 0-89137-437-X

TABLE OF CONTENTS

Introduction

NOW I CAN FLY!

"But ask now the beasts, and they shall teach thee; and the fowls of the air, and they shall tell thee."

—Job 12:7

The sight was a pitiful one. Young birds were flopping in the midst of the sand and debris along the beach. Evidently instinct had prompted the parents to push their offspring out of the birdhouses that dotted the coastline. The young had been nurtured and sheltered long enough. The time for independence had arrived. If the fledglings were going to know the joys of maturity, they had to be forced into a situation that demanded flying for their survival. As I watched this rather common but awesome occurrence of nature, I noticed that several birds flew immediately from the safety of the nest out over the ocean. Others timidly sat on the perch while the parents flew back and forth until enough courage could be summoned. Still others made an effort at the swooping of the wings but landed on the sand beneath the house where danger lurked in the forms of all sorts of predators. Realizing the imminence of destruction, the older birds frantically flew up and down, in circles, and all around their terrified offspring cringing on the ground. They seemed to be saying, "Watch me. This is the way it is done. Come on! Give it a try!" At first, the incident simply seemed interesting to me, but soon grew into one of deep concern as I watched and realized that these precious creatures of nature would either learn to fly or die. It was just as simple as that. Several decaying little bodies along the shore served as grim reminders of the ones who were so fearful that they died from shock, exposure, starvation, or the gnawing of some predator.

I watched and I thought as the waves rolled in and out. I reflected on my own life. In many ways, my years have been like the incident along the shore. When the time came for me to leave the nest and launch out on my own as a full-grown Christian, I was anxious to try. I honestly thought that I could take off across the ocean on the first flutter of wings, but I couldn't. I fell to the ground. After shivering in the cold, after the paralysis produced by internal fear, after being severely wounded by predators, I finally heeded the examples of "how to" from the Master Instructor as my own feelings of self-sufficiency gave way to the admission of inadequacy. Only then could I place my trust in Him, listen to the instruction from His Word, and begin my flight over the ocean with the full assurance that underneath are the everlasting arms.

Faith in **letting go** and completely trusting comes rather easily for some. Most, however, are reluctant learners, and often years slide by as the parts of the puzzle slowly fit together, revealing the shading and blending of various hues. "With the ancient is wisdom; and in length of days understanding" (Job 12:12).

After all the letters and telephone calls from across the nation regarding previous publications, I have reached the conclusion that most of us are basically alike. For the masses who fall into this category, perhaps this work will be of help.

At last I have learned how to fly!

"Underneath are the everlasting arms."

—*Deuteronomy 33:27*

Chapter 1

WHAT'S IT ALL ABOUT?

For most of us, it takes some time to discover the meaning of life.

It seems that some get their acts together when it is just about time for the play to be over. Prayerfully, this book will prevent such a tragedy. I hope that you, the reader, can profit from my mistakes and the resulting lessons that I have learned. Many have followed me all the way from **She Hath Done What She Could**, through **Caterpillars or Butterflies**, and **Let This Cup Pass** to **Meet My Friend David**. I suppose I thought that once anyone has cleared a tremendous hurdle, the battle has been won. I have learned, however, that broken bones can heal much more rapidly than broken hearts. Like practically everyone else in this world, I have had my share of ups and downs since the first publication.

Perhaps the most important lesson which I have learned is that Christians should remove their always-smiling, always-happy, always-untroubled masks. We present a false picture of Christianity when we say we are never frustrated and are always on cloud nine. Such an unrealistic, phony facade drives people away. The world should see beyond our lives to a higher strength. Followers of Christ are not super-fantastic beings, but rather people who are learning and growing each day. Life has not been given to us as a joy ride, but rather as a mission to be accomplished. Never was it promised to be without disappointments or hurts. Putting on Christ is not

11

comparable to putting on a magic shield to protect us from all hurts.

Christians, however, should be more than conquerors (Romans 8:37). While living in the midst of all the problems of this life, we should be the happiest people on the face of the earth. We are triumphant because we have learned the purpose of life. We do not simply wait for an eternal reward for all the hardships and trials endured in this earthly existence. We are joyful right now—this very minute! Such a victory is impossible unless we can learn to fly. Only then can we rise above the muck and mire of life to see the entire landscape below us. Life is made up of highs, lows and level plains. Everyone's life consists of these three basic elements. Your heights, your depths and your smooth points will not coincide with those of mine. Neither will they match those of anyone else. But you will have them. In effect, God is saying, "This is the basic pattern of life. Through its variations, you can either wallow in self-pity or you can live a happy, victorious life. You can fall to the ground or you can learn to fly. The decision is left to you."

LESSONS LEARNED FROM BIRDS

The introduction of this study discussed in detail the incident observed along the beach. Young birds were created to fly. Many, however, were reluctant to rely upon their wings and pitifully fell to the ground, where they summoned enough courage to again try to meet the challenge or else lie there helplessly until some predator put an end to any other chances to use their wings as God intended.

Deuteronomy 32:11,12 speaks of the manner in which an eagle urges her young to take the first leap: "As the eagle stirreth up her nest, fluttereth over her young, spreadeth abroad her wings, taketh them, beareth them on her wings: so the Lord alone did lead him." Note that the mother pushes the eaglets to the edge of the nest and makes them uncomfortable. She may swoop from behind or may even push her offspring out of the nest. In an effort of encouragement, she gives an example by flying around and flapping her wings. On the first flight, the young bird falls through the air on wings never before used. If the fledgling seems doomed, the mother spreads her wings in an effort to catch the fearful off-spring. This process is repeated until the young eagle can fly by himself. "Ye have seen what I did unto the Egyptians, and how I bare you on eagles' wings, and brought you unto myself" (Exodus 19:4).

Isaiah 40:31 also speaks of a lesson learned from the eagles: "But they that wait upon the Lord shall renew their strength; they shall mount up with wings as eagles; they shall run, and not be weary; and they shall walk, and not faint." "Renew" simply means "exchange." We exchange our strength for His strength, and are thus able to soar.

Like the birds, we are fearful of trying, but God never in-tended for us to stay in the nest forever. A few may fly vic-toriously upon the first attempt. Most of us, however, are fear-ful and need additional strength and encouragement to venture out upon God's promises. But remember that God created us to fly. He intended for us to rise above life with all its ups and downs to live victorious, happy years because we know that "underneath are the everlasting arms" (Deuteronomy 33:27).

In the same way that the birds were frustrated, discouraged and paralyzed by fear, so are we. We don't seem to have any concept of what life is all about. Neither are we knowledge-able of God's instructions. Too often, we are tossed back and forth from the extremes of assuming the whole responsibility of our lives with no concept of the grace of God to the opposite position of failure to realize the value of work. Most have never learned to put time in its proper perspective. Too often, we can neither accept God's forgiveness nor can we forgive others. We do not bask in the sunshine of the love of our fellow man. Usually, we cannot offer love to others because we have never learned to love ourselves. Somewhere along the way, we have overlooked the fact that being a good wife and mother is also an important phase of God's work. Somehow, we have failed to learn to rise above strife, and have even become discouraged over inevitable holding pat-terns in the Christian life. We will never learn to fly vic-toriously until we can drop the weights that prevent our fly-ing as God intended.

13

OVERVIEW OF
THE MEANING OF LIFE

Too many have no real concept of Christianity. Christ came that we might have an abundant life (John 10:10). Life is meant to be happy right now! There is an old proverb that wisely observed: "Happiness is a journey, not a destination." Life was never meant to be a merry-go-round of carefree happiness to be enjoyed but rather a responsibility to be assumed. As we trust in God enough to fly, we look back over our shoulders to see happiness flying with us—a deep-seated sense of satisfaction that we are fulfilling our task. We must develop the habit of seeing something positive in everything. Either happiness or unhappiness is a self-fulfilling prophecy. We will find good or bad according to what we expect.

EVERYONE HAS PROBLEMS

Problems are neither good nor bad. They are simply neutral. My attitude toward them determines whether they will weight me down or enable me to develop my wings to the point that I can fly. So often, we become completely engulfed in the problem and can see nothing good in the situation. We have felt like the writer who penned these words:

> Lord, I'm drowning
> In a sea of perplexity.
> Waves of confusion
> Crush over me.
> I'm too weak
> To shout for help.
> Either quiet the waves
> Or lift me above them.
> It's too late
> To learn to swim.

I can understand the desperation of the poet. I have been there, and have felt the same sense of helplessness. Through it all, however, I have learned some great truths about troubles. Perhaps my own weakness has caused me to rely completely upon the strength of God. It seems that most problems fall into one of three categories.

(1) **Problems beyond our control**. The laws of nature are no respecters of persons. A tornado will strike the evil and the righteous. A raging, flooding river is relentless in its destruction. Lightning strikes the most convenient conductor. Fire destroys anything that is combustible. Emotionally and physically handicapped children are born both to faithful Christians as well as the vilest of sinners. Everyone is going to die (barring the second coming of Christ). Illness strikes the elderly and the young, Christians and unbelievers. In fact, statistics show that our bodies peak at about the age of twenty-six and then begin the long degenerative process until we finally succumb to one illness or another.

In addition to the laws of nature over which we have no control, we encounter problems due either to the carelessness or the maliciousness of others. A drunken or irresponsible driver can hit us just as well as anyone else. A criminal will assault or kill one of his vilest associates, or even the most innocent by-stander. Burglars are no respecters of persons when they covet some possession. Those under the influence of drugs can harm with their bizarre behavior anyone with whom they come in contact.

The victorious Christian encounters problems of this nature just as often as anyone else. There is nothing that he can do to change the circumstances. However, with God's help, he can have complete control over his attitude. He accepts the hurdles as inevitable roadblocks in living, and develops spiritual muscles by endeavoring to climb over them, dig under them, crawl around them, or balance them on his shoulders if all else fails. His Christian attitude enables him to put such troubles into proper perspective.

(2) **Problems precipitated by our own carelessness.** We may blame our misfortunes upon God. However, if we are completely honest, we will have to admit that we bring many of them upon ourselves. Our carelessness may be responsible for our home's

15

being destroyed by fire. Failure to heed the speed limit or observe a stop sign may result in a disabling automobile accident. Carelessness could also well be the culprit for any sort of accident that disables or takes the life of a loved one, or even ourselves. Ignoring common rules of good health can so weaken our bodies that they are much more susceptible to disease. The list is endless.

Our own carelessness not only brings about **physical** problems, but the wrong attitude may also precipitate **emotional** hurt as well. People usually find what they are looking for. If our minds have been conditioned to see only the bad in everything that comes our way, we will usually fail to find the nugget of gold buried deeply inside every burden. We may constantly live in the past, imprisoned by circumstances that should have long ago been laid to rest. We may have such a poor concept of ourselves that we emit negative thought waves to everyone with whom we come in contact. We do not love ourselves, so naturally we cannot love others. If other people feel unloved by us, then they will not accept us with warm, open arms. We feel further rejected and send out even more negative waves. The cycle becomes vicious. We may have allowed ourselves to become so bogged down with the cares of this life that we succumb to the ravages of stress. We may be such perfectionists that we can tolerate no faults in others and thus alienate ourselves from the comforts of friendships. Because we cannot accept the grace of God in our lives, we are so burdened by feelings of guilt that we can forgive neither ourselves nor others. We stand in life as a miserable island. We may have been negligent in the training of our children or in the construction of a strong marriage and must consequently bear the heartbreak of wayward children or a broken home. Our own mismanagement of money can be responsible for every sort of materialistic problem. Failure to see the good in troubles and a heavy dose of self-pity may warp our personalities into cynical, irritating, cantankerous people with whom no one can get along. Rather than blame God for the problems which we have precipitated, we

16

should step back and take an objective look at ourselves.

(3) **Problems caused by sin.** Although many of the troubles discussed in the previous section are actually caused by sins of the heart, to an extent they are found in the lives of practically every Christian. Gross sins recognized by any court in the land will also inevitably bring about misery. Murder, adultery, child abuse, lying, stealing, illegal use of drugs and a host of sins in this category can only produce miserable lives.

SOLUTIONS TO PROBLEMS

The first step in dealing with any problem is to admit that it is there. It is not there to be carefully nurtured as the basis of self-pity, but instead it is there to be dealt with. Emotions never die, regardless of how deeply we try to bury them. We should be big enough to say, "I have a problem. It may be something over which I have no control and I must learn how to gracefully accept it, or else it could be caused by my own carelessness or wrong attitude." It is better to admit the problem and recognize natural, legitimate suffering. It was Carl Jung who said, "Neurosis is always a substitute for legitimate suffering." Sometimes, the neurosis becomes more painful than the real problem.

After I admit that I have a problem, I should be objective about it. An infection can never be healed by the application of a bandage. Somehow, the cause of the malady must be cleansed or cut away. The process may be painful, but it is necessary if victorious living is to be expected. Looking deeply within calls for stronger glasses than most of us are willing to wear.

Expect to find a solution. If you don't, you won't. The answer may result in a complete removal of the problem. It may involve a compromise. It could necessitate a mature acceptance of the inevitable. However, we must believe that with God's help, we can handle anything. "I can do all things through Christ Jesus who strengtheneth me" (Philippians 4:13).

Don't be afraid of work. Nothing great in life was ever achieved without effort—a lot of effort. The answer may not be easily found, but it is there if we are willing to honestly search for it. Never automatically accept failure.

Learn to understand the reasons for problems. Even Christ learned obedience from the things which He suffered, not **in spite** of them (Hebrews 5:8). So do we. Accept God's promise in Romans 8:28 at face value. All things **will** eventually **work together** for good for faithful children of God. Climbing over the hurdles in life produces strong emotional and spiritual muscles. Learn to thank God for the rocks. Strong winds produce deep roots for survival. Deep roots produce beautiful trees. "The fining pot is for silver, and the furnace for gold: but the Lord trieth the hearts" (Proverbs 17:3). Realize that God is more interested in what is happening **to us** through our trials than in the **relief** of those burdens. Then, **"Why me?"** becomes **"Why not me?"** as we slowly build our spiritual shock absorbers. We can see further through tears than a telescope as we learn to look upon problems as the dawn instead of the twilight. We learn wisdom from failure much more than from success.

> *"Troubles are often the tools by which God fashions us for better things."*
>
> —*Henry Ward Beecher*

> *"Those things that hurt, instruct."*
>
> —*Benjamin Franklin*

The key. The key to any problem lies within our attitudes. William James, the noted psychologist, observed: "The greatest discovery of my generation is that human beings can alter their lives by altering their attitudes of mind." The writer of Proverbs had discovered that truth centuries earlier when he penned: "As he thinketh in his heart, so is he" (Proverbs 23:7).

We make our own emotions. A problem is neither good nor bad. Our reaction to that problem determines whether it will cause us to become better or will totally destroy our usefulness as human beings. The same event may cause anger in one person and amusement in someone else. Another hap-

18

pening may crush one person, and yet be the basis for the developing of strength in another. Oddly enough, our physical systems work in direct proportion to our emotions. Those working with astronauts in Houston discovered that nausea, sweating and vomiting in space could be controlled in 75% of the cases by influencing the emotions through biofeedback and relaxation techniques. Since we make our own emotions (which, in turn, affect every aspect of our lives), the key to living victoriously in the midst of inevitable troubles lies within each of us. We simply have to be willing to search diligently for the key. With the help of God, we can all find it.

Rocks in the road of life are not problems—they are simply challenges.

LIFE HAS ITS HIGH POINTS

Just as every person's existence has its low points, so does it also have its peaks. While writing this chapter, I originally used the term **prosperity** to describe this part of life, but that particular word has many different connotations. To some, it simply means money and material possessions. To others, it implies a successful, prestigious career. Many consider a prominent social status to be synonymous with prosperity. Money, career and prestige have absolutely nothing to do with the peaks in a person's life. Perhaps the terms "good times, clear sailing, or the absence of serious problems" better convey the real meaning. We are very simply talking about the times in life when practically everything seems to be going well. Money may be plentiful or the bank account may barely stretch to make ends meet. The house or apartment may either be elaborate or small and unpretentious. The job may be prestigious or menial. The clothes may be bargains or designer fashions. However, life is generally smooth. There are no serious emotional or spiritual problems. All seems to be going well.

Such a situation may appear to be good, but it is not conducive to the development of the spiritual muscles needed to fly victoriously. We will never develop our wings as long as we are contented in the nest. Sometimes, we need the high points in life in order to balance the low ones. A constant

19

barrage of troubles will pull most of us under the current. While the low points, or times of problems and decisions, are necessary for the developing of our spiritual muscles, too many could completely destroy us. In His wisdom God is, in effect, saying, "You have gone through many hard times. Now is the time for life to seem good to you. This is a time for you to catch your breath."

While the high points in any person's life are necessary in order to survive, they should be approached with caution. So often, when things go well, we tend to feel that we are self-sufficient and lose our ability to rely upon the strength of God. In that sense, this period of time can also become a severe test. It has been said that if you really want to test a person's character, give him prosperity. It has also been said that adversity will check the depth of stability, whereas prosperity is the test of our integrity.

LIFE HAS ITS LEVEL GROUND

Life has its low points when it seems that everything goes wrong. In His infinite wisdom, God knows that we will never develop our spiritual muscles without them. Life also has its high points. We may have an abundance of material possessions, a prestigious career, fame and a prominent social position; or we may have little of this world's goods, a menial job, and no worldly prestige. The basic core of the high points in anyone's life is the absence of any serious problems. Things are going well for us.

On the other hand, everyone experiences periods of time which could best be described as level ground. The bottom has not fallen out of our world. Neither could we say that all is going well for us. It is the in-between time of life when things are neither all rosy nor all black. It is a mixture of both good and bad with neither one gaining preeminence. True, there are ripples in the sand; but they are minor vexations.

Sometimes we can handle these trivial irritations without any trouble. At other times, they can become a major threat. The wise author of the Song of Solomon, in the 15th verse of the second chapter, admonishes us to beware of the little foxes that can spoil the vines. It is these trivial vexations that can gnaw away at our inner beings until we can be completely destroyed. They are not big problems. In fact, they seem so trivial that we usually feel it is unnecessary to bother God with these tiny vexations. We think that we are big enough to handle them ourselves. This can be our downfall. Whenever we think that we are so self-sufficient, we had better beware! Our downfall can lie just around the bend in the road. Unless minor vexations are handled in the right manner, they can smolder deep within our very beings until our lives become poisoned. We would all do well to heed Solomon's advice and beware of the little foxes that can creep into our lives.

THORNS

Little things.
Things that prick, penetrate
. . . and progressively poison.
Unexpected things.
Low-lying vines that trip, tangle
. . . and eventually imprison.

The thorns which I have reaped
are of the tree
I planted! They have torn me,
and I bleed.
I should have known what fruit
would spring from such a deed.

—Byron

CONCLUSION

I have been the bird on the sand. With the publication of **She Hath Done What She Could**, I suppose I thought that I could fly from the nest without any trouble. Through **Caterpillars and Butterflies**, **Let This Cup Pass** and **Meet My Friend David**, I have experienced my share of struggling to fly, falling to the ground and rising again only to find that my wings were not strong enough. There have been times of songs in the night. "Where is God, my maker, who giveth songs in the night" (Job 35:10). "Yet the Lord will command his loving-kindness in the daytime; and in the night his song shall be with me" (Psalm 42:8). In addition to the low points, there have also been periods of high peaks in addition to the level ground with its minor vexations. Through it all, I feel that I have learned some very valuable lessons as I have grasped the entire scope of life. Through this study, I hope that my struggles will be of some help to ëach of you. Perhaps the words will strike chords of human hearts that will cause them to vibrate for centuries.

I suppose I had once thought that we should struggle through hardships here on this earth and one day be rewarded in Heaven. I doubt that I ever even bothered to thank God for the little thorns that came my way. Looking back over the years, I am sure that I took the high points of life for granted. With the gaining of wisdom, I have learned that we mount to Heaven primarily on the ruins of our cherished dreams as we find that our failures are the rocks we climb upon. Happiness and peace are not reserved for later—they are intended to be enjoyed today! A Christian's life is meant to be victorious, happy and joyful right now—this very minute!

For years, I have treasured the thoughts penned below. Our daughter cross-stitched the words, and they hang as a priceless possession in our home.

What we are is God's gift to us.
What we become is our gift to God.

—Louis Nizer

SUGGESTIONS FOR CLASS DISCUSSION

(1) Should a Christian wear a smiling mask all the time? Discuss the pros and cons. What are the advantages and disadvantages of allowing others to see that we are human and capable of experiencing the normal range of emotions?

22

(2) Apply the training of young birds in the art of flying to the living of a Christian life.

(3) As one rises above the vicissitudes of life, what are the three major types of experiences that are evident in the lives of almost everyone? Why is it so difficult to see a pattern of life when we are so engulfed with daily living?

(4) Everyone has highs, lows and level plains in life. That is what life is all about. Think back over your own life and see if you can discover your own pattern. (This is personal and need not be shared in a class discussion. However, if some desire to do so, the sharing of experiences can be valuable to others who are simply treading water at this moment.)

(5) What thoughts come to your mind when you read of the abundant life in John 10:10?

(6) How can a feeling of happiness or unhappiness be a self-fulfilling prophecy? Don't we usually find what we are looking for—either good or bad?

(7) In this chapter, the statement was made that problems are neither good nor bad—simply neutral. Do you agree or disagree? What role does attitude play? Give concrete examples, either from your life or the lives of others.

(8) What are the three main categories into which problems usually fall?

(9) What are some problems that arise from the laws of nature?

(10) What are some of the troubles brought about by the carelessness or maliciousness of others?

(11) How can a Christian woman be victorious in the midst of problems over which she has no control?

(12) How can our own carelessness bring about many troubles?

(13) What part does the wrong attitude have in the developing of many of our problems?

(14) Some troubles are caused by the laws of nature and the carelessness of others. Others result from our own carelessness or wrong attitudes. Still others are the fruits of sinful living. Cite examples of problems inherent in the last category.

(15) What are the five steps to finding solutions to most problems?

(16) How is our own attitude the key to any problem?

(17) How do we make our own emotions? Give specific examples, especially in relationship to the effect that our emotions have upon our physical well-being.

(18) "Rocks in the road of life are not problems—they are simply challenges." Do you agree or disagree?

(19) When the word "prosperity" is mentioned, what thoughts come to your mind? Discuss the connotation of **prosperity** that has nothing to do with material possessions, achievements, or social status.

(20) Why is the rest of relief found in the high points of life necessary for survival? What can be the dangers?

(21) Solomon warned of the dangers of little foxes in the Song of Solomon 2:15. From your own experiences, what are some little foxes that can cause ripples in the sands of level ground? How have you coped with them?

Chapter 2
THE FLIGHT PLAN

No commercial airplane would consider taking off from an airport until it had first received instructions from the control tower. By means of radio, the pilot and the official on the ground communicate with one another to be certain that everything has been cleared and there are no obstacles to a safe take-off. Long before a pilot takes control of an aircraft, he has mastered the knowledge necessary for flying.

The instructions are not quite so sophisticated, but a similar scene is enacted when a young bird lifts its wings to fly over the ocean. The mother tirelessly gives directions to her young as she swoops around him with fluttering wings. Through her actions and sounds, she gives instructions to the fledgling. Although the sounds mean nothing to us, they are very important to both the mother and her offspring. It is a wise bird who realizes that he is dependent upon his parent for proper guidance. Smug self-confidence could very well cause him to start over the deep ocean before he observed the flight instructions.

People are basically no different from birds or airplanes. Before anyone can live victoriously, he must cease to rely upon himself and trust in God. Over and over, the Scriptures stress the importance of God's instructions:

(1) "Hear instruction, and be wise, and refuse it not" (Proverbs 8:33).

(2) "Receive my instruction and not silver; and knowledge rather than choice gold. For wisdom is better than rubies" (Proverbs 9:10,11).

(3) "Hear, ye children, the instruction of a father, and attend to know understanding" (Proverbs 4:1).

(4) "A wise son heareth his father's instruction" (Proverbs 13:1).

TRUST PRECEDES LISTENING TO INSTRUCTIONS

It is only human nature to ignore the advice from someone in whom we have no trust. We learn to trust in different ways. Some accept God's promises without question. Others doubt and require much soul-searching before they can believe. There is still another group that must be knocked to its knees before belief is possible. Whatever it takes, it is impossible to fly victoriously until one has learned to trust in God enough to read His instructions.

Just as the parent assures the young bird to only trust and do as he is told, so does God admonish His children over and over to simply believe in Him and do as He says.

(1) "As for God, his way is perfect: the word of the Lord is tried: he is a buckler to all those that trust in him" (Psalm 18:30).

(2) "I will never leave thee, nor forsake thee" (Hebrews 13:5).

(3) "Trust in the Lord with all thine heart; and lean not unto thine own understanding. In all thy ways acknowledge him, and he shall direct thy paths" (Proverbs 3:5,6).

(4) "The Lord is my helper, and I will not fear what man shall do unto me" (Hebrews 13:6).

(5) "What time I am afraid, I will trust in thee" (Psalm 56:3).

(6) "Behold, God is my salvation; I will trust, and not be afraid" (Isaiah 12:2).

(7) "Blessed is the man that trusteth in the Lord, and whose hope the Lord is" (Jeremiah 17:7).

(8) "For I am persuaded, that neither death, nor life, nor angels, nor principalities, nor powers, nor things present, nor things to come, nor height, nor depth, nor any other creature, shall be able to separate us from the love of God, which is in Christ Jesus our Lord" (Romans 8:38).

(9) "I can do all things through Christ which strengtheneth me" (Philippians 4:13).

The reader can supply many more verses that assure us of God's care if we will only trust in Him and heed His instructions. Some have found these Scriptures through an organized study of the Bible. Others have discovered them as they groped for strength while drowning in a sea of perplexity.

Regardless of the manner in which we have learned these eternal truths, we should remember that we and God are greater than anything that can happen to **any** of us.

There is nothing wrong with doubting. It can either be powerful or debilitating. In like manner, it can either be crushing or instrumental in developing spiritual muscles. Trust or confidence in God is not the same as self-confidence. It is not cleverness. It simply means to be secure, to have the assurance that, in some way, all things will work together for good.

Underneath are the everlasting arms (Deuteronomy 33:27). We are always in the grasp of God's hands.

(1) "Yea, I will uphold thee with the right hand of my righteousness" (Isaiah 41:10).

(2) "In whose hand is the soul of every living thing" (Job 12:10).

(3) "Behold, I have graven thee upon the palms of my hands" (Isaiah 49:16).

Because the way is dark, we ask for light. Instead, God often gives us His hand.

TWO WAYS IN WHICH
WE RECEIVE GOD'S PROMISES

Teach me thy way, O Lord,
And lead me in a plain path.

—*Psalm 27:11*

God's Word instructs. "I will instruct thee, and teach thee in the way which thou shalt go" (Psalm 32:8). Before the cross of Christ, God instructed His people either directly or through one of His chosen messengers. His wishes were made known to Adam and Eve on a one-to-one basis. Noah was told how to build the ark by God Himself. Abraham, Isaac, Jacob, Moses, Joshua, the judges and the prophets all received divine messages. After the death of Christ on the cross and the completion of the perfect law of liberty, God today instructs us by means of the written word (2 Timothy 3:16,17; 1 Corinthians 13:10; James 1:25). Most of us will very quickly quote Romans 10:17 ("Faith cometh by hearing and hearing by the word of God") to an unbeliever. We assert that the truth shall make us free (John 8:32). Confidently, we proclaim that the Gospel of Christ is the power of God unto salvation (Romans 1:16). No one will be instructed what he should do to be saved directly by God today. It has to be gleaned from a study of the Scriptures.

Too often, we fail to completely accept this great truth at face value in living the victorious Christian life. Just as the Bible is the only source of information to which an unbeliever can go to learn what he must do to be saved, so is it God's book of instruction to each of His children. "For when for the time ye ought to be teachers, ye have need that one teach you again which be the first principles of the oracles of God" (Hebrews 5:12). God's Word is powerful! Within its pages can be found all the instructions needed in order to learn how to fly. Too often, it could be said of us, "Ye do err, not knowing the Scriptures" (Matthew 22:29). Christ answered Satan with the Word (Matthew 4). Peter's remembrance of the Word of the Lord brought him to repentance. That Word is so powerful that our lives can be completely changed. Receiving instruction from the Bible involves more than the ability to quote book, chapter and verse. It is not the number of verses that one can quote nor the amount of sermons one has heard that can make the difference in living as God would have us live. In order to live victoriously, those principles must permeate our beings until they become a part of us and transform our lives.

God instructs us through His Word. What power is contained within the pages of inspiration!

We plead God's promises through prayer. "Be anxious for nothing; but in every thing by prayer and supplication with thanksgiving let your requests be made known unto God. And the peace of God, which passeth all understanding, shall keep your hearts and minds through Christ Jesus" (Philippians 4:6,7).

I have been a Christian for many years, but I honestly believe that I learned more about the meaning of prayer through listening to tapes of the lessons which Ted Kell presented in the Sunset School of Preaching than in any other study. His lessons were based upon a statement which he had heard many years earlier: **"Prayer is simply pleading God's promises."**

> *"What things soever ye desire, when ye pray, believe that ye receive them, and ye shall have them."*
>
> —Mark 11:24

(1) **"What things soever ye desire . . ."**—Note that "what things soever" means all things. This thought is reinforced in John 14:13 *(and whatsoever ye shall ask in my name, that will I do, that the Father may be glorified in the Son)*; in John 15:7 *(If ye abide in me, and my words abide in you, ye shall ask what ye will, and it shall be done unto you)*; and later in John 16:2 *(Hitherto have ye asked nothing in my name: ask, and ye shall receive, that your joy may be full)*. "What things soever ye desire" simply means "whatever you want."

(2) **". . . when ye pray, believe that ye receive them . . ."** involves an understanding of the word "believe." The true meaning of this word can best be understood by examining the manner in which it is exemplified in the lives of men such as Abel, Noah, Abraham and Moses. These men very strongly be-

29

lieved that God would do whatever He promised. Whether the promises were contingent upon offering the right sacrifice, building a gigantic boat according to specifications, leaving home for a faraway land that had been promised, or going before Pharaoh to demand the release of people held in slavery, these men of God believed that the Almighty would do whatever He had promised to do.

God has made certain promises to us just as He did to His servants of long ago. These men pleaded God's promises. Whatever they requested, if it had been promised by God, then it would be granted through prayer. God has promised faithful Christians an abundant life (John 10:10). The means of achieving that life are clearly stated in the Scriptures. We cannot ask for His promises if we do not even know what they are. The only way that we can learn is through His Word.

(3) **". . . and ye shall have them"**—Ask what you want based upon the belief that God will do whatever He has promised. God had promised a propitiation for sin, not the removal of a cup of suffering and agony. God's answer to Christ was "No, I have not promised what you desire." However, God was faithful to His promise.

Prayer is simply pleading God's promises. We desire and ask, believing that God will do what He has promised. We cannot ask for His promises if we do not know what they are. The only way that we can know is through a study of the Bible. It is as simple as that.

Christ's followers asked their Master, "Lord, teach us to pray" (Luke 11:1). We are all children of God by faith in Christ Jesus (Galatians 3:26). The model prayer in Luke 11 speaks of "Our Father, which art in heaven." In agony, Christ addressed God in the garden as "Abba, Father." "Abba" is a tender form, much as we would use the term "Daddy." Since we are God's children, we could very simply say that prayer is a conversation with our father. A child does not have to be told to talk to his parents. It is perfectly natural for him to run to them throughout the day whenever there is happiness to be shared or tears that need to be wiped away. Consequently, prayer is not a duty, a ritual that must be performed at the end of every day. Instead, it is a way of life, a habit.

(1) "Pray without ceasing" (1 Thessalonians 5:17) means exactly what it says. As God's children, we talk to Him constantly—throughout the day. When we are happy, we share the joy with the Father that very minute. When we do something wrong, we do not wait until a dutiful prayer before we go to sleep. (We may not even live until the end of the day to ask God's forgiveness.) Right that minute we pause, admit our shortcoming and ask God's forgiveness.

(2) The habit of prayer is firmly established as part of our emotional makeup. When Christ faced impending death, He followed His regular custom of going to the garden to pray. "And he came out, and went, as he was wont, to the mount of Olives" (Luke 22:39). When Daniel faced a crisis, nothing could change his habit of prayer. After the decree concerning prayer was issued, Daniel prayed "as he did aforetime" (Daniel 6:10), not simply to plead for God's help in an emergency.

Prayer gives us the wisdom to follow the instruction found in the Word of God. "If any of you lack wisdom, let him ask of God that giveth to all men liberally, and upbraideth not: and it shall be given him" (James 1:5). There is a vast difference between knowing the promises and commands of God and in following them.

Prayer is a means of acknowledging our dependence upon God and verbally expressing our needs. "Let us therefore come boldly unto the throne of grace, that we may obtain mercy, and find grace to help in time of need" (Hebrews 4:16). God knows what our needs are, but it is good for us to express them. First, it strips us of pride and promotes humility as we recognize that only God can grant our requests. Secondly, expressing our requests specifically in words enables us to know whether God's answer is "yes" or "no." When we ask, "God, help my child be a better Christian," the plea is so general that it is difficult to know whether God has answered our prayer in the affirmative or not. However, when we plead, "Father, if this job or this move is best in the development of my child's spiritual welfare, please allow things to work out. If it is not beneficial, please make it impossible." With specific requests, we can easily know exactly what God thinks is for our betterment. His verdict is then easier to accept. In Luke 11:5, the man did not simply request food from his friend. He was specific. He said "three loaves." Christ did not pray that God would make His apostles better men. He called Peter by name and asked God to fulfill a specific need (Luke 22:31,32). In Ephesians 6:18-20, Paul asked the saints to pray that he would be able to speak boldly.

Prayer is more than simply expressing a specific request. It also involves merging our wishes with God's will.

Throughout the years, sages have captured within the bonds of words beautiful thoughts concerning prayer:

> *"Prayer is the time exposure of the soul to the highest power that we know."*
>
> —*Harry Emerson Fosdick*

> *"God warms his hands at man's heart when he prays."*
>
> —*John Mansfield*

> *"Prayer is need finding a voice. Prayer is embarrassment seeking relief. Prayer is friend in search of friend. Prayer is a quest in the darkness of midnight. Prayer is the knocking of a barred door."*
>
> —*Ralph A. Herring*

But the best definition of all is simply, "Prayer is pleading God's promises."

CONCLUSION

Every Christian would like to live the abundant life that God has promised. None of us could ever hope to fly victoriously as long as we self-sufficiently flop on the sand. God has given specific instructions for all of us. They are found within the covers of His written Word. We can never fly until we heed the instructions and plead those promises through prayer. The lessons that follow will help us better understand what God's instructions are. With a fuller understanding, hopefully we can have enough courage to ask God to do what He has promised.

SUGGESTIONS FOR CLASS DISCUSSION

(1) Relate the manner in which an airplane and a young bird are able to leave the ground in flight. What is the basic element required of them and also of us if we are to fly victoriously?

(2) Discuss these Scriptures that stress the importance of God's instructions: Proverbs 8:33, Proverbs 8:10,11, Proverbs 4:1, and Proverbs 13:1.

(3) Trust in God must come before we are ready to listen to His instructions. What are some of the various ways in which we learn to trust?

(4) Assign each of the nine passages cited on trust to different members of the class for discussion.

(5) Is there anything wrong with doubting? In what ways can it be powerful? How can it crush us?

(6) What is the difference between confidence in God and confidence in ourselves? Is there anything wrong with self-confidence?

(7) Read the passages that refer to the grasp of God's hands (Isaiah 41:10; Job 12:10; Isaiah 49:16). What special tenderness is denoted?

(8) We receive the instructions for an abundant life through a study of God's Word. We plead God's promises through prayer. During Old Testament days, how did God make His wishes known to His chosen people? Give specific examples.

(9) Today, how does God instruct us? (Note 2 Timothy 3:16,17, 1 Corinthians 13:10, and James 1:25.)

(10) We steadfastly maintain (and rightfully so) that only the Word of God can tell the sinner what to do to be saved. What is the only manner in which a Christian can learn to live victoriously?

(11) We pray for the peace of God mentioned in Philippians 4:7 but often fail to notice the preceding verse to learn the means of securing that peace. What is the prerequisite?

(12) In Mark 11:24, what does the term "what things soever we desire" mean?

(13) In the same verse, what do the words "when ye pray, believe that ye receive them" mean? Contrast belief that we will receive whatever we want with belief that God will do what He has promised.

(14) In the garden, did Christ receive what His human body desired? Why?

(15) What is your opinion of the statement that prayer is simply pleading God's promises?

(16) Discuss two reasons for the benefits derived from specific instead of general requests. Encourage class members to give their own personal examples.

(17) What is your opinion of the statement, "Prayer is more than simply expressing a specific request. It also involves merging our wishes with God's will"?

Chapter 3
FOLLOW
THE COMPASS

The great thing in the world is not so much where we stand as in what direction we are moving.

—*Oliver Wendell Holmes*

The beginning of this study discussed the plight of the pitiful young birds who were struggling on the beach. One of the difficulties was due to the fact that the poor creatures really did not seem to know where they were going or what they should be doing. We, too, struggle and flutter on the ground of life without flying victoriously because so often we do not have the vaguest idea of what a victorious Christian life is all about.

All too often we are much like the driver of the horse-drawn carriage hired to get Thomas Huxley to a certain destination in a hurry. After a short time, the famous lecturer realized that they were headed in the opposite direction. When he asked the driver, "Do you know where you are going?" the latter replied, "No, your honor! But I am driving **very** fast!" We may chuckle at the story, but it is a perfect parallel of most of our lives. We are **very, very** busy; but, all too often, we have absolutely no idea of where we are going. We are so busy with the daily demands that we have no time to pause and ask ourselves if all our frenzied activities are in any way related to helping us become the kind of people we hope to be one day. In fact, far too many of us have absolutely no concrete idea of what we even hope to become!

The ultimate goal of every Christian is eternal life in Heaven, but what are our goals for the kind of life we hope to live here on this earth? To simply say that we hope to become a better Christian, a better wife, or a better mother is far too vague. Every dream, every possibility has simple steps that lead to its development. Our goals must be just as specific as the steps necessary for their attainment.

For example, as the bride of a young preacher, I desired to do as much in God's service as I possibly could. That goal was too general—too vague. Quite frankly, it was frustrating. However, it did give me the opportunity to try my hand in a number of different fields; but I soon learned that I could not do everything. More and more, I found that I gained a deep sense of satisfaction in writing in the field of Christian literature. The goal became more specific. However, I had no real depth at that point. If I had succeeded then, undoubtedly I would have thought that I had done it, that I had brought it about and reached achievement. In His providential love and care, God answered that prayer—not by immediate success, but by allowing me to experience some difficult times on a number of occasions. Struggling through them and search-ing for answers developed spiritual muscles as I learned that I was totally inadequate and that all my strength came from a higher source. I was allowed the privilege of searching and groping for answers until those thoughts became so impor-tant that they had to come out in the form of words. I also learned that you don't write a book just because you **feel** like working on it. You set aside a block of time each day, and those hours receive top priority. Allow me to use this study as a specific example. Early in the fall, I was requested to have a manuscript along this line of thought finished by the end of the following summer. I was in the midst of teaching first-graders in a public school situation in order to send our children to a Christian college. Anyone who has ever taught school will agree that it is difficult to be creative at the end of the day after being in the classroom with twenty-five precious wiggle worms for seven hours. I could not be creative, but I could devote an hour each day to reading, research and note-taking. That meant each Monday through Friday of **every** week. Saturdays provided the opportunity for five or six hours at the typewriter. The only exceptions were the times when our children were home for visits or when I was out of town on a limited number of speaking engagements. The goal was specific—a book on a certain subject by a specified deadline. All too well, I understood what tasks were necessary if that goal were to be reached. I had to work in clearly defined steps as if all depended upon me while at the same time studying and praying as if everything depended upon God. Perhaps such a personal illustration will enable the reader to understand what is meant by a clearly defined goal and the realization of the small steps necessary in achieving that goal.

DEFINITION

A goal is simply a mental image of something that we very strongly desire to come about. In addition to visualizing that goal, there must also be a realization of the necessary steps required to bring that dream to fruition.

IMPORTANCE

Wise men have always recognized the importance of goals. Lack of an ideal can only lead to failure. "There is no more miserable human being than one in whom nothing is habitual but indecision" (William James). "No wind blows in favor of the ship that has no point of destination" (Montaigne).

Generally speaking, we are going to get out of life exactly what we expect. If we expect nothing, then we will receive nothing.

In the secular realm, goals or ideals—both good and bad—are masters of the world.

Think of all the havoc which resulted from Hitler's obsession to rule the world and eradicate a race of people. On the other hand, consider the part that Paul's goal to preach the Gospel to the Gentiles had in the spreading of New Testament Christianity.

Paul is an excellent example of the power of discontent. This apostle was not thrust on his road of achievement by an excellent background with all good things happening at the right time. It was Saul who staunchly stood in the way of Christianity by dragging early converts to prison and by holding the garments of those who stoned the first Christian martyr. His encounter with the Lord on the road to Damascus so upset him, however, that a lifetime of sacrificial service could only in some small way make restitutions for all the wrongs he had committed.

> *"Show me a thoroughly satisfied man, and I will show you a failure."*
>
> —*Thomas A. Edison*

OPPORTUNITIES

We do not wait for great opportunities. We make our own as we walk through life. "A wise man will make more opportunities than he finds" (Bacon).

No person sits by the side of the road and waits for someone to drive up and ask him to ride to a rich, full life. In fact, the one who waits until circumstances are fully favorable will never accomplish anything. There are so many dormant qualities that lie within each of us. There is an old Chinese proverb that says, "All the flowers of tomorrow are in the seeds of today." Any opportunity is worth to a person exactly what his frame of mind enables him to see. "For the ideal with which you go forth to measure things determines the nature, as far as you are concerned, of everything you meet." Unfortunately, opportunities are much like grains of sand in the hands of a child at the seashore. So often, they fall through the hand, one by one, until they are gone.

It has been said that opportunity comes to all, but she has hair in front. Behind, she is bald. If you seize her by the hair, you may hold her. If she escapes, then no one can catch her again. Opportunities to live a richer, fuller life come to us in so many disguises. Because they are wrapped in ugly brown paper instead of beautiful decorative trimmings, too often we kick them out of the way without ever being aware that we have just cast aside an opportunity to become a better person. We may ask for the virtue of patience and then cast aside the opportunity which God allows to come into our lives simply because it hurts us to even look at it. "The secret of success in life is for a man to be ready for his opportunity when it comes" (Disraeli).

AIM HIGH

Ah, but a man's reach should exceed his grasp,
Or what's a heaven for?

—Robert Browning

It was Henry Thoreau who wisely concluded: "Men are born to succeed, not to fail." Wherever we are, it is the starting point for any place that we want to go. Aim at the sun. We may never reach it, but the arrow will fly higher than if aimed at a lower object. We are all familiar with the words of Ralph Waldo Emerson: "Hitch your wagon to a star." Indeed, the poor person is not the one who is penniless. It is the one without a dream. Life has little in store for anyone who does not aim for something better. We, as God's creation, have tremendous possibilities. Most of us only achieve a very small fraction of our potentialities. "If we did all the things we are capable of, we would literally astound ourselves" (Thomas A. Edison).

Christians were created for success, not failure. "We are more than conquerors through him that loved us" (Romans 8:37). "I can do all things through Christ which strengtheneth me" (Philippians 4:13).

"Have a purpose in life, and having it, throw into your work such strength of mind and muscle as God has given you" (Carlyle).

"Not failure, but low aim is the crime."

—James Russell Lowell

PRACTICAL SUGGESTIONS

Realize that we begin right where we are and then throw every ounce of effort into achieving whatever ideal we have set for ourselves. "This one thing I do" (Philippians 3:13). It is healthy to make a good inventory of ourselves the way we are at this present moment if we do not allow ourselves to become contented or discouraged.

(1) **We should get a good mental image of the kind of Christian we hope to be someday.** Visualize even the most minute detail. Imagine it. Expect it. Prime the pump! Never underestimate the power of the subconscious. Positive resolutions act as magnets. Such resolutions, such determination cause some of the greatest things in life to be accomplished by those of only average ability. I have witnessed this so many times in the public school classroom. Children with the highest abilities often do little to rise to their potentialities. On the other hand, a pupil with only low average intelligence can do astounding things simply because he desires to excel so intently. He has thought and dreamed of himself as doing well for so long that he tends to become as he sees himself. We all tend to become what we think. "For as he thinketh in his heart, so is he" (Proverbs 23:7). It is wise to note that a negative image can also serve as a powerful magnet. Whatever we think we are capable of doing or becoming serves as the ceiling of our achievements.

(2) **We never get a good mental picture by negative thoughts.** For example, we do not become a more patient Christian by constantly telling ourselves that we should not be impatient. The house that was emptied of an evil spirit was soon filled with even more evil spirits simply because evil was not replaced with good (Matthew 12:43-45). Neither will saying over and over each day, "I am patient; I am a very patient person," bring about the desired results. We have to be mature enough to read God's Word for instructions and accept the fact that all the tribulations which come our way in life are meant to be viewed as the means of achieving that desired trait of Christianity. "Tribulation worketh patience" (Romans 5:3).

(3) **We should put our goals in writing.** There is something beneficial about seeing anything in

40

writing. Somehow it seems more realistic. We should read over our goals several times each day and think about them as we perform our tasks. Slowly but surely, these dreams or ideals seep into the innermost parts of the subconscious. Once they take root, mighty trees can grow from the smallest seeds.

(4) **Set a time limit!** Vague, fuzzy, "anytime" goals usually amount to very little. There is something about setting a time for achieving an ambition that mysteriously acts as a catalyst to the subconscious mind.

(5) **Work, work, work!** Anything worth possessing requires complete devotion. Jacob, who wanted Rachel so badly that he agreed to work for the seven years which actually amounted to 14, is a splendid example of such devotion. Most of us would literally astound ourselves if we would only be willing to devote the time needed to accomplish nearly any cherished dream. Hearing a great athlete speak of all the hours, days, weeks and years that he devotes to developing a certain skill always puts me to shame when I think of my goals as a Christian. Anything worthwhile requires a lot of scheduled, devoted time.

(6) **Force the actions if necessary.** It's great if the emotions produce the actions necessary for the realization of any goal. If the emotions aren't there, however, the pump can be primed by forcing the actions. For example, someone with an ideal to become an effective Bible teacher may not always be "in the mood" to study for a lesson and make the necessary visual aids needed to get the lesson across. The study may have to be forced, but the ideas and creativity usually follow. The same principle is true in almost every field of Christian service.

(7) **Day by day, we move toward our goals.** As William James so wisely observed, "We forget that every good that is worth possessing must be paid for in strokes of daily effort. We post-

41

pone and postpone until those smiling possibilities are dead. By neglecting the necessary concrete labor and sparing ourselves the little daily tax, we are positively digging the graves of our highest possibilities."

(8) **Goals must be updated.** A person's ideal is much like a horizon. It is constantly receding as he nears it. In fact, anyone will become stagnant if he reaches a goal and then complacently levels off. It has been wisely observed that lofty aims are the wings that help us mount to Heaven. We must learn not to measure ourselves against others, but against **ourselves**. An old proverb from India very succinctly captures this thought in words: "There is no nobility in being superior to someone else. True nobility is in being superior to one's previous self."

> "The rung of a ladder was never meant to rest upon, but only to hold a man's foot long enough to enable him to put the other somewhat higher."
>
> —Thomas Henry Huxley

(9) **Goals will never be reached without a proper perspective of failure.** "In great attempts, it is glorious even to fail." We may never stub a toe by standing still, but we will never go anywhere either. Never allow the "downs" to overcome you nor the "ups" to upset you. Are you growing old or growing up? No one can stay on the mountaintops all the time. There will be valleys all along the way, and we will fall into them from time to time. But we must learn to always climb back up to the higher path that we have selected.

Very few people have ever achieved anything worthwhile until they have first learned to laugh at their own mistakes. There is a vast difference in being able to laugh at one's mistakes and in being irresponsible and flippant. God knows that none of us is perfect. I have always loved the closeness expressed in the words "our voices ring with laughter" found in the song "My God and I."

A Christian who has not experienced that type of companionship has missed one of the greatest joys of this life.

A realization that anyone will stumble from time to time in achieving any goal is a stabilizing force that helps all of us in the development of perseverance. A fire will not burn forever. We must constantly put on fresh logs to keep the flame glowing. It helps to stay away from negative people. Some interaction is necessary if one is to live a full life, but it is indeed foolish to surround one's self with leeches who constantly drain blood from our beings. Keeping a "feel good" file (inspirational writings, notes of encouragement received through the years, etc.) to be pulled out on rainy, blue days can often keep a common failure from becoming permanent.

(10) **We can lose sight of our goals and fall.** It happens gradually. Slowly, we begin accepting things which were previously rejected. Such acceptance is similar to a wedge that is driven into a piece of wood. The opening is very small at first, but gradually it becomes wider and wider.

Paul so wisely admonished the Corinthians, "Wherefore let him that thinketh he standeth take heed lest he fall" (1 Corinthians 10:12). Years earlier, wise King Solomon would have been spared much misery if he had only followed such advice. This chosen ruler exceeded all the kings of the earth in riches and wisdom (1 Kings 10:23). Slowly, he began to compromise his principles as he allowed his wives to lead him into idolatry. At his death, mighty Israel was left in ruins—confused and torn asunder in civil war.

It has been discovered that a frog can be killed without a struggle by simply placing it in a beaker of cool water over a low flame. The temperature of the water is raised so gradually that the poor creature can be cooked in approximately two and one-half hours while he placidly sits there, barely blinking his eyes and never even trying to jump out. We chuckle and pity the intelligence of the frog, but Israel gradually wandered from God and was admonished by Jeremiah to wake up and see its fallen position (Jeremiah 2:2-8). Christians today are a lot like frogs.

WHAT IS
A VICTORIOUS CHRISTIAN?

As I have been sitting here at the typewriter while working on this chapter, one thought has constantly run through my mind: "How can I give a thumbnail sketch of the qualities possessed by a victorious Christian?" How are we going to know what our goals are if we do not have in mind a clear picture of the person we hope to become?

I turned to the Book of Matthew and slowly read it through, making a notation of every trait of character that it admonished. By the time I had reached the conclusion of the 25th chapter, I had written 59 characteristics ranging all the way from being humble, loving one's enemies and being a quiet yet powerful influence to brazenly standing for the truth, even against father or mother.

Then I made a list of some of the attributes of God and found these:

(1) Repented and grieved over the making of man (Genesis 6:6)

(2) Grieved over rebellion (Psalm 79:1-13)

(3) Showed wrath and displeasure (Psalm 2:5)

(4) Laughed at enemies (Psalm 2:4)

(5) Anger (Jeremiah 7:18,20)

(6) Joy (Isaiah 62:5)

(7) Love (John 3:16)

(8) Vengeance (Deuteronomy 32:35)

(9) Hatred of images (Deuteronomy 16:21,22)

A study of the feelings of Christ indicated these:

(1) Compassion (Matthew 9:36)

(2) Anger (Mark 3:5)

(3) Capacity to weep (Luke 19:41; John 11:35)

(4) Agony prior to the cross (Luke 22:44)

44

(5) Love—tender affection implied (John 20:2)

(6) Deeply perturbed and moved as He groaned in the spirit (John 11:38)

(7) Sighed in His spirit (Mark 8:12)

(8) Cried out on the cross (Matthew 27:46)

(9) Sorrowful, heavy in spirit (Matthew 26:37,38)

(10) Joy (John 15:11 and 17:13)

(11) Loneliness (Matthew 26:40-45; John 6:15; Luke 9:18)

(12) Control of emotions (1 Peter 2:23)

(13) Stricken, smitten, afflicted (Isaiah 53:4,5)

After my own personal study, I reached a conclusion. It is impossible to give a detailed description of a victorious Christian. Each of us is different. Each has his own set of natural strengths and weaknesses. Paul, the well-educated, highly influential Jewish leader who changed from the persecutor to the persecuted, developed into an entirely different type of Christian from the rugged, impulsive fisherman Peter who vacillated from denying the Lord to boldly proclaiming Him on Pentecost. Yet each man was precious in God's sight as his own set of natural characteristics yielded to the touch of the Master Potter to become different yet powerful forces in spreading the Church in the first century.

If you were to sit down and make a list of all the Christian characteristics that you would like to ultimately develop, in many respects your list would differ from mine because you and I are distinct individuals. There would be a common core with many variations. We will never reach all of them, but we will achieve far more than if we merely wander aimlessly.

To every man there openeth
A way, and ways, and a way.
And the high soul climbs the high way.
And the low soul gropes the low.
And in between, on the misty flats,
The rest drift to and fro.
But to every man there openeth
A high way and a low,
And every man decideth
The way his soul shall go.

What is your decision?

SUGGESTIONS FOR CLASS DISCUSSIONS

(1) Give a simple definition of a goal in life.

(2) Do you agree or disagree with the statement, "Generally speaking, we are going to get out of life exactly what we expect"? State your reasons.

(3) How did Paul's discontent thrust him on his ultimate path in life?

(4) How do opportunities usually come to us?

(5) Booker T. Washington wisely observed, "Success is to be measured not so much by the position that one has reached in life as by the obstacles which he has overcome while trying to succeed." What are some of the obstacles that a Christian may encounter without ever even realizing that such problems are, in reality, opportunities?

(6) In setting goals for our lives, what is the value in aiming high? What can be the hindrances?

(7) Paul said, "This one thing I do," in Philippians 3:13. What is your one central aim in life?

(8) Usually we tend to become the personification of the mental image that we have of ourselves. With this thought in mind, where should the changing of a person begin?

(9) Why do negative thoughts fail to produce a positive image?

(10) What is the value of a written goal? Have you done any writing lately?

(11) Give a concrete example of setting a time limit on a goal.

(12) Most of the worthwhile things in life seldom just happen. They are products of dreams with foundations of diligent, hard work. How much work was Jacob willing to invest in Rachel? Compare this to the amount of time we are usually willing to invest in achieving something that is desired.

(13) What is the value of forcing the actions if necessary?

(14) Give examples of the "strokes of daily efforts" that are necessary in the achieving of any dream.

(15) As we move closer to the realization of a goal, why is it necessary to update that desire? What will happen if we fail to do so?

(16) Failures will inevitably come. How can we prepare ourselves so that a stumble will not knock us off our course?

(17) Most people do not relinquish their ideals suddenly. The death of such dreams comes slowly. Relate the incident of the killing of the frog in a beaker of water. What dreams have you allowed to die in a similar manner?

(18) Trace the steps in the fall of King Solomon.

(19) Allow me to challenge you to go through the Book of Matthew (or any other of the Gospels) and make a list of the characteristics of a follower of Christ.

(20) Describe Paul as a mature Christian. Do the same for Peter. How do the two men compare as paragons of Christianity? How do they differ? What is the lesson for each of us?

(21) Now that you have concluded the study of this chapter, spend 15 minutes a day for a week in actually writing your own personal goals for a victorious Christian life.

Chapter 4
WORK IS GOOD FOR YOU

Do not ask for a talent. Instead, ask for the wisdom to desire a noble purpose and the strength to persevere in taking the daily small steps necessary to achieve that ambition. Success, like sand, can slip through the fingers unless it is held tightly by consistent hard work—day in and day out, year in and year out.

No one has ever lived a victorious Christian life by accident. It comes as a result of many factors, one of which is the urgency to persevere until a well-defined goal has been reached. However, no person has ever lived victoriously by sheer determination to get the job done. We work as if everything depends upon us, while at the same time we throw ourselves completely upon God's mercy. We could never work hard enough to earn our salvation, but God does require diligence upon our part before His mercy is extended.

SCRIPTURAL ADMONITIONS FOR DILIGENT WORK

The Scriptures abound in admonitions for diligent work. Over and over, from the earliest days of inspired writing through the completion of the New Testament, God admonishes His children to work, work, work.

   (1) "The way of the slothful man is as a hedge of thorns" (Proverbs 15:19).

(2) "And in every work that he (Hezekiah) began in the service of the house of God, and in the law, and in the commandments, to seek his God, he did it with all his heart, and prospered" (2 Chronicles 31:21).

(3) The description of the worthy woman in Proverbs 31 is an excellent example of industry.

(4) In Proverbs 6:6-11, the sluggard is admonished to consider the industrious ways of the lowly ant.

(5) "By much slothfulness the building decayeth; and through idleness of the hands the house droppeth through" (Ecclesiastes 10:18).

(6) "The soul of the sluggard desireth, and hath nothing: but the soul of the diligent shall be made fat" (Proverbs 13:4-6).

(7) The Thessalonians were commanded to work if they expected to eat (2 Thessalonians 3:10).

(8) In the parable of the talents, the slothful servant who fearfully hid his one talent was severely rebuked (Matthew 25:14-30).

(9) "And let us not be weary in well doing: for in due season we shall reap, if we faint not" (Galatians 6:9).

(10) "Therefore, my beloved brethren, be ye steadfast, unmovable, always abounding in the work of the Lord" (1 Corinthians 15:58).

(11) "Preach the word; be instant in season, out of season" (2 Timothy 4:2).

(12) Diligence is certainly implied when Paul spoke of striving, running and fighting (1 Corinthians 9:25-27).

(13) The parable of the leaven clearly defines the type of quiet, consistent work expected of God's workers (Luke 13:20,21).

(14) "Love not sleep, lest thou come to poverty" (Proverbs 20:13).

(15) "Seest thou a man diligent in his business? he shall stand before kings" (Proverbs 22:29).

(16) "If any provide not for his own, and specially for those of his own house, he hath denied the faith, and is worse than an infidel" (1 Timothy 5:8).

(17) Probably the Scriptural commands for diligence are best summarized by the sage in Ecclesiastes 9:10: "Whatsoever thy hand findeth to do, do it with thy might."

WORLDLY ADMONITIONS

After reading the verses cited in the previous section of this lesson, there can be no doubt about God's commandments to work diligently and consistently.

In the secular world, even men with no religious convictions have long recognized the necessity of industry. In my studies, I have made a collection of such insights. Although these statements cannot be placed on the same level as divine commands, they are still food for thought.

(1) "The expectations of life depend upon diligence; the mechanic that would perfect his work must first sharpen his tools" (Confucius).

(2) Even the worldly, wicked Napoleon recognized the value of work—"Victory belongs to the most persevering" and "The truest wisdom, in general, is a resolute determination."

(3) "It is better to wear out than to rust out" (Cumberland).

(4) "Though you may have known clever men who were indolent, you never knew a great man who was so; and when I hear a young man spoken of as giving promise of great genius, the first question I ask about him always is, 'Does he work?' " (Ruskin).

(5) "I am convinced that that which makes the difference between one man and another—between the weak and powerful, the great and insignificant, is energy—invisible determination—a purpose once formed, and then death or victory. This quality will do anything that is to be done in the world; and no talents, no circumstances, no opportunities will make one a man without it" (Buxton).

(6) "Great opportunities come to all, but many do not know they have met them. The only preparation to

take advantage of them is simple fidelity to what each day brings."

(7) "Great things are done when men and mountains meet" (William Blake).

(8) "Some are the victims of what happens. Others are the masters."

(9) "The hero is no braver than an ordinary man, but he is brave five minutes longer" (Ralph Waldo Emerson).

(10) "O Lord, Thou givest us everything, at the price of an effort" (Leonardo da Vinci).

(11) "To reach the port of Heaven we must sail, sometimes with the wind and sometimes against it. But we must sail or lie at anchor" (Oliver Wendell Holmes).

(12) "If you have great talents, industry will improve them; if moderate abilities, industry will supply their deficiencies. Nothing is denied to well-directed labor. Nothing is ever to be attained without it" (Sir Joshua Reynolds).

PRACTICAL SUGGESTIONS

As Christians, far too many of us never get off the ground, much less fly, simply because we are unwilling to put forth the necessary effort. We are lazy. We procrastinate. We don't intend to be failures—we simply lack the ambition to be successful. Frequently, we don't even read the instructions diligently. So often, we only half-heartedly try to put those God-given principles that we do know into effect. Perhaps the following practical suggestions will give us the courage needed to try our wings.

(1) Don't be content merely to just live. Attack life with vigor.

(2) Diligent work does not depend upon moods with their ups and downs. It is not done in spurts but is consistent.

52

(3) Work is firm. It does not back down. It is faithful, reliable, trustworthy and solid.

(4) Diligent attention to detail is the key for turning something ordinary into something great. Diligence and discipline are the parents; consistency is the child.

(5) Hard work becomes a habit. Each day, we weave a thread of it until the rope becomes so strong that we cannot break it.

(6) Victorious people often begin their success where others end in failure.

(7) Daily effort spent on a desired goal may seem insignificant. However, if one walks vigorously three hours a day, in seven years he will walk a distance equal to the circumference of the globe.

(8) We realize the value of the maxim "use it or lose it" in dealing with the building of physical muscles, but somehow tend to forget the same principle in spiritual matters.

(9) "Laziness grows on people. It begins in cobwebs and ends in iron chains. The more one has to do, the more he is able to accomplish."

(10) Only the disciplined are free.

(11) Luck is spelled "W-O-R-K."

(12) Frequently, we do well in endeavors that require the use of our natural talents; but we usually excel in those that cause us to overcome our deficiencies.

(13) Almost all works of greatness are the result of perseverance. Think of all the strokes required in the building of the great pyramids of Egypt.

(14) Attitudes must be changed before the vast strength of determination deep within us can be tapped.

(15) The dictionary is the only place where success comes before work.

(16) Hard, consistent work is not enough. It must also be enthusiastic. Hard work alone has the connotation of monotomy, weariness, drabness. We must get excited about a victorious Christian life.

"Nothing great was ever achieved without enthusiasm" (Ralph Waldo Emerson). Enthusiasm can be learned. William James had some excellent advice: "If you want a quality, act as if you already have it. Act as if you have plenty of enthusiasm."

(17) Enthusiasm is not only contagious, it is also healing. "A merry heart maketh a cheerful countenance; but by sorrow of the heart the spirit is broken" (Proverbs 15:13). "A merry heart doeth good like a medicine: but a broken spirit drieth the bones" (Proverbs 17:22).

MAKING THE APPLICATION

At this point, there should be no doubt in the reader's mind that hard work is necessary for success in **anything**, but even more especially in the living of a Christian life. We have found abundant admonitions from the Scriptures. For centuries, sages of the world have recognized the essentiality of diligence. Many practical suggestions have been offered. Now let's make the application personal.

I can be complacent and flutter on the ground until I am overcome by one predator or another, or I can desire to fly victoriously so badly that I am willing to back off and see the true meaning of life. Any life—that of a Christian or an unbeliever—is going to experience its share of good times, despair and normal days. The difference is the ability of the child of God to realize where he is going and to have the determination to tenaciously "hang in there" until he achieves his dreams.

A diligent disciple prays persistently. The story of the importunate widow (Luke 18:1-8) teaches that more is required than a flippant "help me live a better Christian life" prayer. We must specifically pray for each virtue that we hope to have in our lives, for each person we hope to convert, and for the forgiveness of particular sins. Over and over, day in and day out, we lay our supplications at the throne of God.

A victorious Christian realizes that a knowledge of the truth is gained by diligent study. Bible study is hard work. Daily, the determined Christian gleans the gems of wisdom found within the pages of inspired writing. Constant, diligent thought must be given to the material studied as he slowly meditates upon it and allows the wisdom to sink into his heart.

A sincere child of God is never satisfied until he has probed deeply within to uncover the reasons for his wrong attitudes. He persistently searches his own heart until he clears all the deeply-hidden muck and rottenness that prevent the growth of a proper Christian outlook. Sometimes such a search may require many years and tears, but he stays with the problem until—with God's help—he is the victor.

A soul winner is diligent in searching for the lost. He is so disturbed over the millions who die unprepared each year that he is constantly searching for receptive hearts and is willing to devote the time required for teaching God's Word. He has no magic formula. He simply loves the lost and is willing to invest any amount of energy necessary to reach an honest hearer. He will find a way—**some** way.

Teaching God's Word is so important and so exciting that a true follower will invest hours in study and preparation. He is so well prepared and so filled with the Word of God that he teaches from the overflow. If a visual aid will help the learner remember the lesson, then hours spent on such activities seem as minutes.

Diligent, hard work is required in every facet of the Christian life. Most of us do not reap the dividends because we are too slothful to invest the necessary time.

As long as we are willing to try and will work diligently, God is much like a parent or a teacher who hovers over a child learning to write. He lovingly guides our fingers while whispering words of encouragement: "Keep trying. Don't quit."

SUGGESTIONS FOR CLASS DISCUSSION

(1) If you had a choice, would you ask for a talent or a great purpose in life? State your reasoning.

(2) Will our work alone insure our salvation? What else is required?

(3) In every work, King Hezekiah did it with all his heart (1 Chronicles 31:21). Review the major events in this ruler's life.

(4) In what ways did the worthy woman of Proverbs 31 show industry? What is the implied lesson for us?

(5) The industrious ways of the ant are extolled in Proverbs 6:6-11. Have one class member do some research on the work habits of this creature.

(6) Try to find a picture of the house described in Ecclesiastes 10:18.

(7) If the Thessalonians expected to eat, what were they commanded to do (2 Thessalonians 3:10)?

(8) What wrong did the servant with one talent commit (Matthew 25:14-30)? In what ways are we like this man?

(9) How can we become weary in well-doing (Galatians 6:9)?

(10) Discuss the quiet work of leaven (Luke 13:20,21). What does this mean in a Christian's life?

(11) According to 1 Timothy 5:8, who is worse than an infidel? In what ways is he worse?

(12) Apply Ecclesiastes 9:10 to various phases of a Christian's life.

(13) Under the section entitled "Worldly Admonitions," assign each one to be read aloud by a different class member. Solicit their comments.

(14) Do most Christians intend to be failures? What is one of the most predominant reasons for becoming lukewarm?

(15) How do we go about making hard work a habit?

(16) Can we always control what happens to us in this life? How can we be masters of situations over which we have no control?

(17) Have you personally known of someone who has made a success of what most people would term a failure in life? Share the experience with the class.

(18) Draw an analogy between failure to use physical and spiritual muscles.

(19) Hard work alone is not enough. It must be enthusiastic. What difference does enthusiasm make?

(20) Apply the dimension of hard work to each of these phases of a Christian life:

> prayer (Luke 18:1-8)
> Bible study
> cleansing of wrong attitudes
> searching for the lost
> teaching God's Word

(21) Add other spiritual areas in which success is spelled "W-O-R-K."

Chapter 5
I'M IN LOVE WITH ME

Mary avoids other people. They have hurt her in times past, and she fears further rejection. Instead of opening her arms in genuine love to them, she has surrounded herself with a thick protective emotional shield. Although she may not recognize the feelings, deeply buried inside lie anger, guilt, and even resentment. She has a negative self-image.

Mary has a low self-esteem. She does not love herself.

Mary's case is not uncommon. It has been estimated that at least three-fourths of the people in this nation do not have a positive image of themselves.

Inner feelings of inadequacy and self-criticism may find outward expression in different ways.

(1) June may wallow in self-pity by constantly running herself down, belittling her abilities, complaining that she can't do anything right, and also by giving negative reactions to compliments.

(2) This same feeling of inadequacy may seek to protect itself in an entirely different manner. Instead of seeming to be shy and withdrawn, Ann may mask her feelings by constantly striving to appear better than anyone else, by trying to make herself seem important to people, by bragging, by trying to impress others, by being argumentative and complaining, by endeavoring to be a perfectionist in order to be impressive, by depending upon personal achievements for a sense of worth, by overeating, by being

loud and boisterous, and by having a strong drive to control others. There is a general feeling of anxiety and lack of peace.

These totally different personalities stem from the same problem—none has a healthy love for self.

BIBLICAL COMMAND

Matthew 22:35-40 records the incident of the lawyer's trying to tempt Christ with the question, "Master, which is the great commandment in the law?" The Son of God replied:

(1) Thou shalt love the Lord thy God with all thy heart, and with all thy soul, and with all thy mind.

(3) Thou shalt love thy neighbor (2) as thyself.

Sometimes we tend to get these commands out of sequence. We readily admit that we should love God first, but in our minds we usually place the emphasis on loving others next.

It is impossible for anyone to properly love his neighbor unless he first loves himself. There is a vast difference between healthy self-love and the arrogance spoken of in Romans 12:3 when Paul admonished the Christians there not to think of themselves more highly than they ought to think. True self-love finds expression in deep humility.

THE TERMS

A real understanding of self-love (or self-esteem) is impossible without a proper grasp of some terms.

(1) **Self-image** is the way you **see** yourself. In your mind's eye, you may view yourself as a beautiful person or be painfully aware of some physical flaw.

(2) **Self-confidence** is one's belief in an ability to perform in certain areas. For example, I may have no faith in my ability to ski, yet this awareness of a fact does not have to lower my opinion of myself.

I simply have to be mature enough to realize that no person can do all things well. I may not be able to ski, but I can do other things better than the most able skier in the nation.

(3) **Mirrored image** is simply the picture of myself as it is reflected from others by the tone of their voices, their glances, their touch. There are so many ways in which a person tells me that he likes me, he has no use for me, or he considers me as neutral. He doesn't like or dislike me. I am simply of no consequence in his opinion. Naturally, my self-image, my self-confidence, and even my self-esteem are affected by what I sense in my reflection from all those with whom I come in contact.

(4) **Self-esteem** is the way I **feel** about myself as contrasted with the way I **see** myself in my self-image. Self-esteem is the value that I place upon myself. It is the conclusion that I have reached about myself in my mind. I may be fully aware that I am not beautiful or even have some outstanding physical flaw. I may recognize the fact that I am totally inadequate in performing many activities. But I can still have a healthy self-esteem. In spite of all my shortcomings, I can still value myself very highly. Self-esteem and self-love are synonymous with one another.

A number of years ago, I talked with a woman who was severely critical of others. No person ever did anything right in her eyes, and she very quickly made her viewpoint known. In an effort to understand the reason for such criticism and bitterness, I sat down and talked with her at length. During the course of the conversation, she made the statement that she seldom did anything right herself and could not understand why other people could not see all their own faults. Then I understood her bitterness and critical attitude. She did not love herself, and consequently could not love others. Centuries ago, Christ said that no one could really love his neighbor until he first loved himself. The Son of God knew all about the value of self-esteem long before the term ever existed.

BIBLICAL REASONS FOR SELF-LOVE

Each one of us is precious in the sight of God. In the very beginning God said, "Let us make man in our image, after our likeness . . . So God created man in his own image, in the image of God created he him; male and female created he them" (Genesis 1:26,27). His evaluation of His creation is given in the 31st verse of the same chapter: "And God saw every thing that he had made, and behold, it was very good."

Through the years, even though man sinned and did many terrible things, he still remained precious in the opinion of God. The Father loved us so much that He gave His only begotten Son in a horrible death in order that man might have eternal life (John 3:16). Peter emphasized the great price which was paid for our redemption: "the precious blood of Christ, as of a lamb without blemish and without spot" (1 Peter 1:19). Not only were we bought with a great price, but we remain special to the Creator. Paul's epistles are filled with words of rebuke and correction for the wrongs committed by the first Christians, yet God did not count them worthless. Over and over, He chided His children to repent, but He loved each one.

Since God has placed such a high value on the worth of each of us, **we** should love ourselves if **He** loved us that much.

PHYSICAL RESULTS

Both the emotional and physical makeup of human beings are so intertwined that a lack of self-love, or self-esteem, is reflected in each. Many of the emotional consequences were discussed in the introduction of this chapter. The physical body also suffers.

The internal fear, conflict, and anxiety that naturally result when we are down upon ourselves trigger a multitude of physical reactions as well. Such a state of mind can cause an increase in hormones and abnormal toxins from the pituitary, thyroid and adrenal glands.

The body has both a parasympathetic nervous system, which maintains the functioning of the body in a relaxed or normal maintenance state, and a sympathetic nervous system, which increases bodily functions when we are in a troubled or negative state of mind. The adrenal glands pour out adrenaline, and the production of other hormones is increased by the reacting pituitary-adrenal-cortical system of the brain. Such bodily functions are necessary when there is immediate danger (such as an encounter with a rattlesnake), but they can be fatal if they continue over an extended period of time.

The emotional system controls by:

(1) **Regulating the amount of blood going to the various organs.** Dilated blood vessels are manifested in blushing when someone is embarrassed. On the other hand, tightened blood vessels are frequently the cause of severe headaches.

(2) **Affecting the secretions of some glands.** For example, the dry mouth often experienced by public speakers is triggered by a decrease of the saliva glands. Emotions can stimulate an excess of thyroxin from the thyroid gland, resulting in toxic goiter. The adrenal glands, if overstimulated, can result in high blood pressure, arthritis, kidney disease, and hardening of the arteries.

(3) **Tension of the muscles.** This affects the muscle tone of the entire body. Tightened neck muscles and involuntary contractions of the muscles in the intestines are but two examples.

It can readily be seen that we must learn to develop a wholesome love or respect for ourselves if we are to enjoy the benefits of good health.

CAUSES OF
A LACK OF SELF-LOVE

A lack of love for self can be traced to a number of different causes.

Part of a lack of self-esteem may find its roots in an **inherited temperament** (inborn traits that subconsciously affect one's behavior). For centuries, different personality types have been recognized. No person is one of those types exclusively but usually leans toward one. These temperaments have the technical names of sanguine, choleric, melancholic and phlegmatic but can be more easily understood by the terms personable, hard-driving, gifted-artistic and easygoing. Some are born with an inherited temperament that makes them more loving and outgoing which, in turn, causes them to feel good about themselves, and consequently they are able to hold themselves in better esteem. On the other hand, others are naturally more melancholy, moody and withdrawn. While such individuals appear to be aloof and calloused, they usually have a strong desire to be loved. Their inability to attract the friendship of others lowers their own self-esteem.

Perhaps it would be wise at this point to clarify three terms:

(1) **Temperament** results from inborn traits.

(2) **Character** is developed as basic inborn traits are influenced by early childhood experiences, taught principles, and the manner in which one interprets the surrounding world.

(3) **Personality** may or may not be the real person. Often, an individual may act the part of what he thinks he should be according to acceptable conduct.

Early childhood experiences leave an indelible impression upon the mind of a youth. A child has no reasoning ability. He reacts either positively or negatively according to what is fed into the subconscious mind. He does not realize that certain negative emotions of childhood (such as envy, anger, or jealousy) are normal reactions. Feelings of guilt over these emotions result from an inability to reason maturely. If a person is constantly run-down, criticized, shamed, insulted and seldom praised, then naturally he develops a low opinion of himself. Sometimes parents or others may not be guilty of these things but still are too busy or unknowledgeable of the importance of developing a child's self-esteem to invest the time and attention needed to develop this most important concept in a young mind.

Rejection by a child's peers can be devastating. Anyone who has spent time working with young children knows how painfully cruel they can be to one another.

In addition to an inability to reason (and consequently a distorted view of right and wrong), constant criticism from parents or other authority figures and rejection by peers, a child's self-esteem may be lowered by his physical environment (run-down house, unattractive clothes, lack of money or education).

The key to anything that happens in a child's life is his attitude toward the circumstance or event. If the child is aware of the contrast in his own life style and that of others, usually the four experiences discussed above are damaging to a youngster's healthy love of himself. Sometimes, however, he may be so repulsed by them that they can actually be a springboard to developing a good self-esteem as the child struggles to rise above any undesirable circumstances. **Attitude is the answer.**

> *If a child lives with hostility, he learns*
> *to fight.*
>
> *If he lives with criticism, he learns*
> *to condemn.*
>
> *If he lives with fear, he learns to*
> *be apprehensive.*
>
> *If he lives with jealousy, he learns to hate.*
>
> *If he lives with self-pity, he learns to be sorry*
> *for himself.*
>
> *If he lives with acceptance, he learns to love.*
>
> *If he lives with fairness, he learns justice.*
>
> *If he lives with honesty, he learns what*
> *truth is.*
>
> *If a child lives with friendliness, he learns*
> *that the world is a nice place in which*
> *to live.*

Later experiences after childhood can also cause a lack of self-love in anyone.

(1) **Teenage peer pressure** is intensive. A dominant characteristic of this age in life is acceptance. It is this trait, more than any other single factor, that

causes teenagers to abandon moral values taught since earliest years. They must already have a healthy love of self to avoid being swept under these strong waves of pressure.

(2) **Marriage experiences** can either make or break an adult's value of himself. The blending of two in this sort of lifetime partnership affords maximum opportunity for steadily increasing or decreasing a person's sense of worth. Marriage also seems to serve as a fertile field for the growth of childhood hurts that have lain dormant for years.

(3) **Failure in a career** is an important factor in the way that a person values himself. It takes a strong sense of self-love to withstand the loss of a job or the social prestige that usually accompanies a prominent position.

(4) **Parenthood** can also be a cause of the failure to have a healthy self-esteem. Unless a young adult, especially a young mother, has a mature outlook on life, the inevitable failures and frustrations of rearing young children can make any parent question her own sense of worth.

Constant feelings of guilt naturally will cause anyone to have a low opinion of himself. A realization of guilt is necessary for the salvation of everyone. Wrongs must be confessed and corrected or we will be lost eternally. Some are so calloused that nothing seems to phase their sense of guilt. There are many others, however, who are so conscientious that they can never seem to forgive themselves, even after they have been forgiven by God. This inability to forgive oneself can only come with a realization of the grace of God (Ephesians 2:8,9).

STEPS TOWARD SELF-LOVE

Since one must love himself before he is capable of loving others, and since this is one of the three most important commandments in the sight of God, every Christian should come to the sobering realization that he must take whatever steps are necessary to develop a healthy love of self.

(1) **Realize your value in God's sight.** You were created in the image of God (Genesis 1:26,27). That creation was valued as good (Genesis 1:31). Since Christ loved us enough to die for us (Romans 5:8), we should not constantly belittle ourselves.

(2) **Be willing to examine your life, thoughts and feelings. Then, be honest enough to pull the problem into the open.** The answers usually lie within ourselves if we will only stop and think. It was Socrates who said, "Know thyself."

(3) **Ask yourself how many times you have allowed the same bad, traumatic thoughts to run back and forth through your mind until they have formed deep ruts and have become habitual ways of thinking.** Watch your thought patterns (especially the negative ones) and analyze them before such thinking can become a neurosis.

(4) It was William James who drew the valid conclusion that the most exciting discovery of our generation is the fact that **we can alter our person by altering our attitude of mind.** Long before this noted psychologist lived, the wise writer of Proverbs captured the same thought in the words, "For as he thinketh in his heart, so is he."

(5) **Realize that people have different temperaments.** To be different is not to be inferior.

(6) **Accept the fact that you are not perfect.** A forgiven sinner, yes; a perfect Christian, no. The whole duty of man is to fear God and keep His commandments (Ecclesiastes 12:13), but it is impossible for anyone to keep every commandment perfectly. We must do all that is within our power, and then rely upon the grace of God to help us the rest of the way.

(7) **Make a conscious effort not to criticize yourself constantly.** You cannot extend love and compassion toward others unless you can first accept it yourself.

(8) **Each time a critical thought comes into your mind, replace it with a positive statement**

about yourself. Make a list of your good points. Form a mental picture of the positive image.

(9) **Avoid living in the past with all the bad things that have happened to you.**

(10) **Try to develop a thicker hide regarding criticism from others.** Realize that anyone who tries to do anything **will** receive criticism. (Most people criticize without thinking.) Also, be aware of the fact that a critical person usually feels inferior, and this is his way of building himself up. Be careful yourself not to repeat anything bad that someone has said about another—it can be crushing to the one criticized.

(11) **Accept the fact that you are worth something as a PERSON, not because of your successes or your approval from others.**

(12) **If certain people or circumstances seem to be lowering your self-esteem, try to avoid them as much as possible.**

(13) **Make a conscious effort to love others and make them feel good.** (You may have to prime the pump if you do not first love yourself.) This action will, in turn, cause you to feel better about yourself. It is the best cure for self-pity.

CONCLUSION

Many different circumstances may contribute to a lack of healthy love for yourself. Ultimately, however, the way you feel about yourself is the result of what you choose to believe. This is the reason that many strong individuals come from rather negative backgrounds.

It was Ralph Waldo Emerson who said, "Self-trust is the first secret of success." George Bernard Shaw was a bit more practical when he wrote, "Better keep yourself clean and bright. You are the window through which you must see the world."

Self-love is not conceit nor arrogance. It is the acceptance of yourself with the same love and tolerance of your shortcomings that you desire God and others to exhibit toward you.

If you can't be a pine on the top of the hill,
Be a scrub in the valley—but be
The best little scrub by the side of the rill;
Be a bush, if you can't be a tree!
If you can't be a bush, be a bit of the grass
And some highway happier make.
If you can't be a muskie—then just be a bass
But the liveliest bass in the lake;
We can't all be captains—we've got to be crew.
There's something for all of us here;
There's big work to do—and there's lesser to do;
And the task you must do is the near.
If you can't be the highway—then just be a trail;
If you can't be the sun—be a star;
It isn't by size that you win or you fail;
Be the best of whatever you are!

SUGGESTIONS FOR CLASS DISCUSSION

(1) Discuss the different manifestations of the same problem presented in the introduction of this lesson. What is the cause of the trouble?

(2) How did Christ answer the question of the lawyer concerning the great commandment in the law? Why do we usually get the last two out of order?

(3) Why is it impossible for anyone to properly love his neighbor unless he first loves himself?

(4) What is the difference in healthy self-love and the arrogance spoken of in Romans 12:3? How does true love find expression?

(5) What is a synonym for self-love?

(6) What are the meanings of the terms "self-image," "self-confidence," "mirrored image" and "self-esteem"?

69

(7) Cite Scriptures that establish the high value that God has placed on each of us. If God loves us that much, why can we not love ourselves?

(8) In what three general ways does the emotional system affect the physical body?

(9) What part can an inherited temperament play in a lack of self-esteem? What are the differences in the terms "temperament," "character" and "personality"?

(10) What is the influence of negative early childhood experiences? Cite four different examples.

(11) What effects can these experiences have upon one's opinion of his self-worth:
(a) Teenage peer pressure
(b) Marriage experiences
(c) Failure in a career
(d) Parenthood

(12) What effect can a lifetime of constant feelings of guilt have upon a person's value of himself?

(13) Under the heading "Steps Toward Self-Love," assign each of the suggestions to a member of the class for discussion. Add others to the list.

(14) Do you agree or disagree with the statement that ultimately the way you feel about yourself is the result of what you choose to believe?

(15) Cite the definition of "self-love" that was given at the conclusion of this study. What is your opinion? Give other definitions.

Chapter 6
I LOVE YOU, TOO

Loneliness is a universal problem. Loneliness is . . .

. . . standing by a freshly-dug grave.

. . . preparing a meal for yourself and going to bed early.

. . . feeling all alone in a crowd.

. . . feeling unimportant.

. . . feeling that others don't care.

Everyone wants someone to love them, to notice them, to make them feel important. Even Christ experienced loneliness and rejection when the Father turned His back on the beloved Son. He was in such agony that He literally screamed aloud (Matthew 27:46).

So many live in prisons of loneliness. "Ninety-nine persons out of every hundred are lonely. And the one who says he isn't probably is" (Paul Tournier, Swiss physician). Psychiatrist Harry Stack Sullivan emphasized the same thought when he observed, "The deepest problems of our society are loneliness, isolation, and the inability to have self-esteem." At the very dawn of time, God recognized this universal problem when He said, "It is not good that man should be alone" (Genesis 2:18).

One of the deepest needs in human nature is the desire to be accepted, to belong. The pain of rejection is one of the hardest to bear. It is much more difficult than body pain or normal sorrow. Many wear a "don't care" mask to cover feelings of rejection. They may even be bitter or withdrawn.

Frequently, the feelings may originate in early childhood and the person will have the scars for life.

So often it is true that the lonely person invites the feeling. It is his own fault. Even though he himself probably craves love and attention, the protective shell of aloofness causes him to seem unlovable; and others generally turn away to a more receptive person. The vicious cycle goes on and on. Generally speaking, the person does not love others because he does not love himself. No one can reap the benefits from loving others until he has first learned to love himself (Matthew 22:37-39). A mastery of the previous chapter must precede a study of this one.

SCRIPTURAL COMMANDS

There can be no doubt about the necessity to develop the capacity to love others. It is essential to our salvation.

(1) "We know that we have passed from death unto life, because we love the brethren" (1 John 3:14).

(2) "A new commandment I give unto you, That ye love one another; as I have loved you, that ye also love one another. By this shall all men know that ye are my disciples, if ye have love one to another" (John 13:34,35).

(3) "But whoso hath this world's good, and seeth his brother have need, and shutteth up his bowels of compassion from him, how dwelleth the love of God in him? My little children, let us not love in **word**, neither in **tongue**; but in **deed** and in truth" (1 John 3:17,18). Note that this can be **any** need that my brother may have, whether it be physical, emotional, or spiritual.

(4) "And this is his commandment, That we should believe on the name of his Son Jesus Christ, and love one another, as he gave us commandment" (1 John 3:23).

(5) "This is my commandment, That ye love one another, as I have loved you" (John 15:12).

72

God not only commanded love for others. He is the supreme example of the depth of that love. "For God so loved the world, that he gave his only begotten Son, that whosoever believeth in him should not perish, but have everlasting life" (John 3:16).

Remember that all the above commands are impossible unless we first love ourselves (Matthew 22:37-39). This is the key that unlocks the door.

UNEXPECTED BENEFITS

The emotional needs of every human being are basically alike. We all need to feel loved and accepted. We cannot feel loved and accepted by most people unless we first love them. Whatever wave length we send out into life will be reflected in our own lives. "As in water face answereth to face, so the heart of man" (Proverbs 27:19). "The world is a looking glass, and gives back to every man the reflection of his own face" (William Thackery).

Psychological reciprocity maintains that if we treat others in the right manner, they will usually respond in kind to us. In other words, we will reap what we sow.

> *There is a destiny that makes us brothers:*
> *None goes his way alone:*
> *All that we send into the lives of others*
> *Comes back into our own.*

> *—Edwin Markham*

We are all bound together on this earth. What affects one affects another.

> *No man is an island entire of itself. Every man is a piece of the continent, a part of the main. If a clod be washed away by the sea, Europe is the less, as if a promontory were. Any man's death diminishes me, because I am involved in mankind. Therefore never send to know for whom the bell tolls. It tolls for thee.*

> *—John Donne*

The shadows of our lives fall across the lives of others. The vibrations of our lives will be felt for years to come.

Happiness if often unexpected. Dr. Albert Schweitzer wrote, "I don't know what your destiny will be, but one thing I know. The only ones among you who will be really happy are those who have sought and found how to serve." Francis of Assisi realized this fundamental truth when he wrote:

> O divine master, grant that I may not so much seek
> To be consoled as to console,
> To be understood as to understand,
> To be loved as to love.
> For it is in giving that we receive:
> It is in pardoning that we are pardoned:
> It is in dying that we are born to eternal life.

Luke 6:38 applies to emotional benefits as well as temporal:

> Give, and it shall be given unto you; good measure, pressed down, and shaken together, and running over, shall men give into your bosom. For with the same measure that ye mete withal it shall be measured to you again.

Happiness does not result from **finding** the right person or people—it comes from **being** the right person.

WATCH THE TONGUE

The tongue can either make or break any desire that one might have in learning to love others. "Pleasant words are as a honeycomb, sweet to the soul, and health to the bones" (Proverbs 16:24). "A merry heart doeth good like a medicine: but a broken spirit drieth the bones" (Proverbs 27:22). "A man hath joy by the answer of his mouth: and a word spoken in due season, how good it is" (Proverbs 15:23). "A soft answer turneth away wrath: but grievous words stir up anger" (Proverbs 15:1). The words which pass from our lips—in addition to a smile, a look, a touch—are so vital in establishing a bond of love between two people.

Words spoken in anger, or even thoughtless and unkind words, can bind our arms as we reach out to others. "The words of a talebearer are as wounds, and they go down into the innermost parts of the belly" (Proverbs 18:8).

So often we hurt others with our words—not because we intend to do so, but simply because we don't know when to close our mouths. "He that hath knowledge spareth his words: and a man of understanding is of an excellent spirit. Even a fool, when he holdeth his peace, is counted wise: and he that shutteth his lips is esteemed a man of understanding" (Proverbs 17:27,28). "He that keepeth his mouth keepeth his life: but he that openeth wide his lips shall have destruction" (Proverbs 13:3).

Watch the **tone** of the voice! It can convey more meaning than the words used.

LOVING THE UNLOVABLE

There is no problem involved in loving a sweet, kind, compassionate person who makes us feel good about ourselves. However, there is a concrete wall between us and the unlovable. We must find a way to climb the wall, dig underneath, or make a passage through it. Sometimes the challenge can be tremendous.

> *He drew a circle that shut me out—*
> *Heretic, rebel, a thing to flout.*
> *But love and I had the wit to win;*
> *We drew a circle that took him in!*
>
> *—Edwin Markham*

Sometimes our pride and fear of being hurt hold us back. Then we are the losers. "Everyone that is proud in heart is an abomination to the Lord" (Proverbs 16:5). "Only by pride cometh contention" (Proverbs 13:10).

Love is the lubrication and may have to be used by the will at first. Also, we must work on our own hearts and realize that we will not let others dictate what our own feelings and emotions will be. We should be mature enough to realize that those who are the most unlovable usually need love the most. They have never known the warmth and release that being loved and accepted can bring. Such people hide behind protective shields in order to defend themselves. Try to walk in their shoes and see through their eyes. "But he that hateth his brother is in darkness, and knoweth not whither he goeth, because that darkness hath blinded his eyes" (1 John 2:11).

Grow up! Leave behind the child whose main emphasis was to be loved, and develop into the mature adult who can give love to others. Be strong enough to take some chances of being hurt. Open your heart!

Developing unselfish love is much like developing a muscle—it must be stretched, exercised and constantly used. Loving others sometimes has to be exercised by the will. "A friend loveth at all times" (Proverbs 17:17). This is the essence of agape love.

Help the unlovable build **bridges** instead of **walls**.

Help them understand that to be rid of loneliness, one must have friendship with God, friendship with self, and then friendship with others (Matthew 22:37-39).

Love God! Love self! Love others!

SUGGESTIONS FOR SHOWING OUR LOVE TO OTHERS

(1) When we love and care for others, we are showing our love for Christ. "Inasmuch as ye have done it unto one of the least of these my brethren, ye have done it unto me" (Matthew 25:40).

(2) We want others to like us, be kind and forgiving, show an interest in us, be understanding, and make us feel important. Most of all, we want them to tell us about our soul's salvation. But we want to be told in a kind, understanding manner. We should do the same for others. "As ye would that men should do to you, do ye also to them likewise."

(3) The same Paul who persecuted the early Christians gave the blueprint for loving others in the 13th chapter of 1 Corinthians:

> Love is patient, kind, not jealous, does not brag or act arrogant, does not behave unbecomingly, is not selfish in seeking its own, is not easily provoked, does not keep a record of wrongs suffered, does not rejoice in seeing others do wrong but rather rejoices in the truth, bears all things, believes in all things, hopes all things, endures all things, never fails.

The opposite is true for those trying to protect themselves from hurt:

pretentious, showy, boastful, impatient, harsh, cold, envious, tactless, blunt, suspicious, quick-tempered, gloating over the hardships of others, pessimistic, fickle.

(4) Be willing to go the second mile. Do more than just what is expected.

(5) Realize that we are all different. Christ, in His immediate circle of twelve, had many personalities. The closest were Peter, James and John. Look at the differences in Peter and John, yet Christ loved both.

(6) Realize that we have a wide circle of people whom we love (some are lovable, some are not). But we have only a few very close friends. Christ only had three. True friendship requires many years of sharing joys and sorrows.

(7) Realize that love for others requires time to grow, much as a seed.

(8) The late Professor William James of Harvard noted, "Action seems to follow feeling, but really action and feeling go together; and by regulating the action, which is under the more direct control of the will, we can indirectly regulate the feeling, which is not."

(9) Find something for which to sincerely compliment three people a day. Everyone wants to feel important in some way. Everyone has a strong point.

(10) Write a note of praise, encouragement, or gratitude to two people a week.

(11) Each week, visit one lonely person.

(12) Plan to fix a dish of food once a week for someone who needs it. Prepare the food one day and drop it by the person's house the next day as you run routine errands.

(13) Listen intently to others as they talk. Make eye contact with one eye. Nod your head. Smile. Don't burden them with your problems. Listen without interruption. Encourage them to talk about themselves. "Keep your fears to yourself, but share your courage with others" (Robert Louis Stevenson).

(14) Realize the importance of your own ego and the ego of the other person. Remember that when this ego is attacked, anyone will fight for its survival.

(15) Whenever you meet a shy person, show a genuine concern and try to discover one thing in which he is truly interested.

(16) Try a smile on someone who appears unfriendly. Take the initiative in developing a friendship.

(17) People like to be called by name. Make them feel important by trying to remember.

(18) Use good manners—"thank you," "please," "would you mind," etc.

(19) Choose your words wisely when you think someone is wrong. Don't be argumentative. Take a firm stand for the truth, but don't constantly be an agitator. This is especially true when trying to teach God's way.

(20) Realize that you are human. Don't set yourself up as being perfect. Admit your shortcomings. Be willing to say "I'm sorry."

(21) Try to step into the other person's shoes and see things from his standpoint. Be sympathetic to his feelings.

(22) Have you ever felt compassion for the lame man who sat by the pool for thirty-eight years and had no friends to help him (John 5:5-9)?

(23) Help a person save face—even when he is wrong.

(24) Notice little things. Be thoughtful.

CONCLUSION

Loving others is simply genuinely caring for them. The essence of what love is all about is summarized in the following story:

> *A little girl was sent on an errand and was late in returning home. Her mother asked her why. She replied that her playmate had broken a doll. She had stopped to help her. When the mother inquired how, the child simply replied, "I sat down and helped her cry."*

SUGGESTIONS FOR CLASS DISCUSSION

(1) On a chalkboard, list many definitions of "loneliness." (Urge the class members to add to the list suggested at the beginning of this lesson.)

(2) When did Christ experience loneliness?

(3) Why is the problem of loneliness one of the most important ones in the world today? How can this be possible when there are so many people? Share experiences of being lonely in a crowd.

(4) What is one of the deepest needs in human nature? Why is rejection so painful?

(5) How does a lonely person frequently invite the feeling?

(6) According to Matthew 22:37-39, what is a primary reason for the failure to love others?

(7) Read and discuss the Scriptural commands for loving others.

(8) What was God's supreme example of love for others (John 3:16)?

(9) When we withdraw into cold, hard shells of protection, what is the image that we emit to others? What sort of feeling is reflected to us? How can the vicious cycle be broken?

(10) What is the principle of psychological reciprocity? Does it seem to make sense to you?

(11) Unfriendliness is really a manifestation of fear and selfishness. Do you agree or disagree?

(12) When we give freely to others, what will happen according to Luke 6:38?

(13) How can **being** the right person be better than **finding** the right person?

(14) Cite Scriptures to prove the benefits of pleasant words.

(15) According to Proverbs 18:8, describe the hurt caused by the words of a talebearer.

(16) How can we hurt others unintentionally simply because we talk too much without being discriminating in our choice of words?

(17) What can the tone of the voice convey?

(18) When someone is unlovable, what is the lubrication that can best be used?

(19) What is your opinion of loving others at first by exercising the will instead of the emotions of the heart? Is this being hypocritical?

(20) Why should we help the unlovable build **bridges** instead of **walls**?

(21) According to Matthew 25:40, what is one way we can show our love for Christ?

(22) How does the admonition in Luke 6:31 (treat others as you would like to be treated) help us show our love for people?

(23) Describe both the positive and negative aspects of love that are implied in 1 Corinthians 13.

(24) Beginning with the fourth suggestion for showing our love to others, assign one to each class member for comments.

(25) Read aloud the conclusion of the lesson.

Chapter 7

CHARIS!
IT'S FREE

One of the primary reasons for so many miserable Christians is the inability to accept the forgiveness of God—to completely understand God's grace. Like the bird, we also flutter on the sand because we are fully aware of our imperfections and yet believe that we must somehow be perfect and do enough good works to merit our salvation. We never seem free from the feeling of guilt.

God's grace is perhaps one of the least understood subjects of the Bible, especially as it pertains to a child of God. We have fought grace versus works for so many years in trying to defeat error that perhaps we have leaned too far to the side of works and have overlooked the assurance of grace. Within the Church today, there is a new trend of "grace only." The teaching is in error but is probably a backlash resulting from the stressing of the importance of works. The purpose of this particular study is to help the mature Christian grasp a deeper meaning of forgiveness, especially as it pertains to the living of an everyday Christian life.

DEFINITION

"Grace" is simply "God's unmerited favor." It's as simple as that.

Grace is primarily a New Testament theme. It is mentioned thirteen times in the Old Testament and 135 times in the New

Testament. Legalism demanded **give me what I deserve; man works and earns his salvation**. The Old Testament was based on legalism, and yet none could be saved.

There is a difference between "mercy" and "grace." "Mercy" says, "You **don't** get what you **deserve**. You **deserve** to go to Hell, but I won't send you." On the other hand, "grace" asserts, "You get what you **need** but don't **deserve**. You **don't** deserve to go to Heaven, but I'll take you."

ALL NEED GRACE

Every person sins each day. Alien sinners commit wrongs and so do Christians.

(1) "For all have sinned, and come short of the glory of God" (Romans 3:23).

(2) "There is none righteous, no not one" (Romans 3:10).

(3) "If we say that we have no sin, we deceive ourselves, and the truth is not in us. If we confess our sins, he is faithful and just to forgive us our sins, and to cleanse us from all unrighteousness. If we say that we have not sinned, we make him a liar, and his word is not in us" (1 John 1:8-10).

However, both the alien sinner and the child of God can be saved. Both groups are saved by the grace of God, and both groups must accept that grace under different conditions.

JAMES 2 AND ROMANS 4

In our study of grace, perhaps it would be best to begin by clarifying James 2 and Romans 4.

James 2 states that Abraham was justified by works. In Romans 4, we read that if Abraham had been justified by works, he had whereof to glory. In other words, Abraham was not justified by works.

The answer is simple when one examines the **kind** of works referred to in each passage. If the reader will only

82

examine the last part of the third chapter of Romans, he will readily see that the works referred to in the fourth chapter are simply the **works of the law**—the law of Moses. Abraham was never justified by the works of the law. He was never even under the law of Moses. Neither were those under the law justified. "Therefore by the deeds of the law there shall no flesh be justified in his sight; for by the law is the knowledge of sin" (Romans 3:20).

On the other hand, the second chapter of James states, "Was not Abraham our father justified by works, when he had offered Isaac his son upon the altar? Ye see then how that by works a man is justified and not by faith only." Clearly the works of James 2 are the **works of obedience**.

Abraham was never justified by the meritorious works of the law of Moses. He died long before the law was given. He was justified by the works of obedience—an obedience that did **whatever** was required of him.

EPHESIANS 2:8,9

The third and fourth verses of the second chapter of Ephesians shed further light upon the grace of God. "For by **grace** are ye saved **through faith**; and that not of yourselves: it is the gift of God; not of works, lest any man should boast."

One might paraphrase these verses by saying, "For by grace are ye saved through faith [belief coupled with obedience according to Thayer]; and that [grace] not of yourselves: it is the gift of God: [grace is] not of works, lest any man should boast."

The only manner in which a person can be saved is by the grace, or unmerited favor, of God. The way that anyone can receive that grace is through faith, or belief plus obedience.

For example, public education is available to all. Everyone is entitled to receive it. Nevertheless, the offer alone is not enough. One has to reach out and put forth both the physical and mental obedience required to receive such a gift.

I had been a Christian for a long time before I ever had any real understanding of the grace of God. When I was injured so critically a number of years ago, I did not deserve to live. The doctors gave no hope. I did nothing to deserve it; but God, in His grace, gave the precious gift of life to me. It was an undeserved gift from Him, but I had to reach out to receive it by struggling to live. There had to be some effort on my part. At that time, the song "Amazing Grace" became popular. How well I can remember crying every time I heard it because the words hit so close to home. When I think I have become self-sufficient now, it takes only the hearing of those words to bring to mind the wonders of the grace of God. I think I had to experience the benefits of grace in a physical sense before I could fully comprehend them in a spiritual manner.

HALL OF FAME

Since Ephesians 2:8 emphatically states that one is saved by grace through faith, it is vital that we understand what the term **through faith** means. The Scripture explains itself if only given a chance. After a close examination of the 11th chapter of Hebrews, there could be little doubt.

Over and over, the famous Bible characters illustrate by their lives that faith is simply a trusting belief in God that compels one to do whatever the Father asks.

Abel trusted in God enough to offer unto the Father whatever sacrifice was demanded. An animal sacrifice might not have made sense; but if that was what God wanted, then His wishes would be fulfilled by Abel.

We are not told exactly what Enoch did in obeying God; but whatever it was, the action was pleasing.

I have often wondered what thoughts must have gone through Noah's mind when he was informed that he would be saved from a tremendous flood if only he would follow God's explicit commands according to the blueprint and type of wood (and it had never even rained before this time!). Noah was saved by grace through faith (belief coupled with obedience).

God's command to Abraham to journey to a country which he had never seen demanded great faith. The offering of his son Isaac, the heir through whom the promises made to Abraham were to be fulfilled, must have been a tremendous test of faith. But that belief in God's grace (unmerited favor) was the basis for Abraham's great faith—a belief so strong that it willingly obeyed whatever God asked, whether it made sense or not.

Don't overlook Abraham's wife—Sarah. It was through faith that Sarah received strength to conceive and deliver a child when she was ninety years old. Any woman can understand what a strong faith Sarah must have had!

The children of Israel really didn't deserve to be freed from their Egyptian masters; but God offered His grace, or unmerited favor. Moses believed in God so strongly that he gave up the pleasures of living in Pharaoh's court in order to lead thousands of mumbling, grumbling, complaining people in the scorching heat of a desert for forty years. His belief was so firm that he instructed the people to do something that seemed ridiculous—the sprinkling of the blood of lambs on doorposts. God extended His grace to the Israelites through their leader Moses. Jehovah's commands may have seemed completely illogical, but Moses' belief was so great that he was willing to instruct his people to do whatever God asked them to do.

Can you imagine the jeers of the inhabitants of Jericho as they watched the children of Israel walk around their city once each day? What sort of military attack could this be? Try to step into the shoes of God's men as they marched not once but seven times on the seventh day. Sense the feeling in their lips as they lifted their rams' horns and blew and then shouted mightily. Can you feel their suspense as the first stone of the city walls began to tremble, and their awe as the entire walls crumbled before their very eyes? They had done nothing to deserve this military victory. Not only did their actions appear to be foolish, but they also allowed themselves to be "sitting ducks" to the arrows of the soldiers of Jericho. God had offered His grace, His unmerited favor. In order to receive that grace, the Israelites had to believe. They did not simply assume that the walls would tumble if they had enough faith in God. That belief had to slip into the sandals that encircled the city each day; that faith had to lift the rams' horns to the lips and blow. That which God had requested may have seemed to be completely illogical, but the people's faith in God's grace to do what He had promised was so great that they were willing to do whatever He required.

This passage goes on to mention the belief of Rahab, Gideon, Barak, Samson, Jephthah, David, Samuel, Isaac, Jacob and Joseph. All these people had tremendous faith. They believed that God would give them something that they did not deserve. That belief in God's grace was so overwhelming that they would do **whatever** God required, no matter how foolish it might have been. None of these people could have received God's unmerited favor if they had not reached out to accept it with hands of obedience. None of the acts of obedience could possibly have earned what Jehovah granted to them; but not one person could have received the grace of God if he had not explicitly followed divine directions, whatever they were.

It is really quite simple.

GRACE TO THE ALIEN SINNER

Understanding the background of the 11th chapter of Hebrews enables one to better comprehend the saving of a sinner. How often have we heard the illustration of the man who is drowning. There is nothing that he could possibly do to merit God's grace—to earn the gift of salvation. Yet God offers salvation by extending the rope of baptism. Man does not deserve to be saved; but God says, "I will extend my grace to you [the gift of salvation] if only you will reach out and grasp the rope offered to you [baptism]." Man is saved by grace through faith (Ephesians 2:8), but that faith must be willing to do whatever God asks.

Most Christians can understand this principle.

GRACE EXTENDED TO CHRISTIANS

Many Christians, however, seem to drop the subject of the grace of God as they shed their wet garments of baptism. From that moment on, so many feel that the only way they can be saved eternally is to painfully earn each step of the way.

Just as God specifically instructed all His children in the 11th chapter of Hebrews, so does He explicitly inform an alien sinner what he must do in order to receive God's grace in salvation. But the Christian is not left alone to laboriously fight for the rest of his life as if salvation depended entirely upon his own works. The child of God will be saved by grace through faith, just as the principle applied to Abel, Enoch, Noah, Abraham, Sarah, Moses and all the other "greats" of the Scriptures. They believed in God's grace so strongly that they were willing to do whatever God asked of them. The terms were different in each instance. Under the perfect law of liberty, God has demanded the same obedience from every alien sinner in order to receive the grace of salvation.

In like manner, the Christian can never do enough to earn his salvation, yet he must believe in God so devotedly that he will do whatever is asked. Certain specifics are given in detail—the organization of the Church and the worship within the framework of that divine institution. By faith, the individual believer complies with **whatever** God has requested. In addition, general commands are given to each Christian. We must study. We must pray. We must visit the sick and care for the physical needs of others. We are admonished to teach the lost, to give of our means, to train our children in the ways of the Lord, and to be a good wife. We must develop our Christian character by adding the Christian graces of love, joy, peace, long-suffering, gentleness, goodness, faith, meekness and temperance.

We can understand the specifics. We know that we must observe the Lord's Supper every first day of the week and that we can make no substitutions for the bread and the fruit of the vine. We accept the items of worship as God required and staunchly defend the purity of these acts. We have no question concerning the blueprint for the organization of the Church.

When we get to the general commands, however, we sometimes become confused. We must study, but how much? Ten minutes a day? An hour? Six hours? We must pray. How often? At bedtime? In the morning? Two minutes? Two hours? We must visit the sick. One visit a week? One each day? Everyone in the hospital? How many lost people must I teach in order to receive God's grace of salvation? One in my lifetime? One a year? One a month? How many hours should I spend in being a good wife? How much time should I invest in training my children? How much love, joy and long-suffering should I manifest in my life? There is so much guilt. There are so many feelings of inadequacy in the lives of many Christians.

In a sense, it seems that it would be a relief if the Father had specifically outlined our responsibilities as He did under the law of Moses. At least they knew how far they could walk on the Sabbath. They knew exactly how much money they had to give. All the sacrifices were explicit. At this point in the stream of time, God was dealing with people who were much like children. Everything had to be spelled out in detail. The death of Christ, however, ended that law and made possible a new law: the perfect law of liberty. And it is just that—a law of liberty. It is encompassed by some very specific commands, and these must not be violated. Within the walls, however, are some general laws of degree. The answer to the perplexing question of how much and to what degree these laws must be fulfilled in order to be pleasing to God is found in the first verse of the 12th chapter of Romans. God only expects our **reasonable service**. What would be reasonable in God's sight for you might not be considered reasonable for me.

God is merciful. He is gracious. We could never do enough to earn the grace of salvation. Just as every obedient one from Abel to the Israelites on the day of Pentecost, we do whatever our Father specifically requires of us, whether it seems to make sense or not. We then follow His general commands to the best of our abilities and with the right attitude, realizing that God only expects our reasonable service.

I am not perfect, and I will **never** be perfect. I must constantly ask for forgiveness as I realize my imperfections and repent of them. I realize that God has given specific commands which I must follow and also many general commands which I gladly fulfill by my reasonable service from a heart overflowing with thankfulness for the grace of God which I could never deserve.

No Christian can live a victorious life if he feels that he must earn every step of his salvation. It is utterly impossible. Such an attitude can only bring frustration to anyone who is honest enough to realize his own inadequacy. By our faith (belief coupled with obedience), we leap into God's arms of grace. A Christian cannot live victoriously until he can completely accept God's forgiveness and, in turn, forgive himself.

AMAZING GRACE

Amazing grace! How sweet the sound,
That saved a wretch like me!

I once was lost, but now am found.
Was blind, but now I see.

'Twas grace that taught my heart to fear.
And grace my fears relieved;
How precious did that grace appear
The hour I first believed!

Thru many dangers, toils and snares,
I have already come;
'Tis grace hath bro't me safe thus far.
And grace will lead me home.

SUGGESTIONS FOR CLASS DISCUSSION

(1) What is grace?

(2) Is grace primarily a theme of the Old Testament or New Testament?

(3) Contrast "grace" and "legalism."

(4) Establish the fact that all are sinners by a discussion of these verses: Romans 3:23, Romans 3:10, and 1 John 1:8-10.

(5) Since the alien sinner and the child of God are both sinners, is each one saved in the same manner?

(6) The second chapter of James states that Abraham was justified by works. The fourth chapter of Romans says that Abraham was not justified by works. How can the two passages be reconciled? What is the difference between the works of the law and the works of obedience?

(7) Read Ephesians 2:8,9. Paraphrase the verses in your own words.

(8) The only way in which a person can be saved is by the grace of God. How is that grace received?

(9) Use the illustration of public education to discuss its availability to all. What must be done before anyone can receive its benefits? Apply this principle to grace.

(10) Assign different class members one of these Bible characters: Abel, Enoch, Rahab, Gideon, Barak,

Samson, Jephthah, David, Samuel, Isaac, Jacob and Joseph. How did each one obey God, regardless of how illogical that command might be? Did any of them **earn** the blessing that they received by their actions? What was the purpose of the actions?

(11) Use the illustration of throwing a rope to a drowning man to illustrate God's grace and man's part in receiving the benefits of that grace. Give illustrations of your own.

(12) Why do so many Christians seem to feel that salvation is totally dependent upon their own good works after baptism? Why is this frustrating?

(13) What are the specific commands required of an unbeliever? What are some specific rules concerning the organization of the Church and the worship required of Christians? Can substitutions be made?

(14) Discuss some general commands given to Christians. To what degree must they be observed?

(15) Romans 12:1 gives the key for carrying out general commands required of all Christians. In following these commands, must every Christian's obedience be identical? Support your reasons.

(16) How can a full acceptance of the forgiveness of God enable one to live victoriously?

Chapter 8

I FORGIVE YOU

"Forgiveness is the fragrance the violet sheds on the heel that crushed it."

—*Mark Twain*

One of the greatest problems facing the Church today is the inability of Christians to forgive one another.

We continue to fight battles that should have ended long ago.

Too many of us collect grievances as we would gold beads that are proudly worn around the neck. We wear them with dignity—much as a badge of heroism. We even take them off from time to time, polish them and gleefully count the number.

It's a bit ridiculous.

We loudly proclaim, "He that believeth and is baptized shall be saved; but he that believeth not shall be damned" (Mark 16:16). If anyone believes and is baptized, he will be saved. If he doesn't, he will be lost. We can't seem to understand how anyone could fail to see the clarity of such a plain and simple command.

The same Bible that emphatically states the fate of one who fails to believe and be baptized is also just as adamant concerning the question of forgiveness.

"And forgive us our debts, as we forgive our debtors . . . For if ye forgive men their trespasses, your heavenly Father will also forgive you: but if ye forgive not men their trespasses,

91

neither will your Father forgive your trespasses" (Matthew 6:12,14,15).

It may hurt to admit something that is so clearly stated. We are all sinners (Romans 3:23; Romans 3:10; 1 John 1:8-11; James 3:2). Not a single person will go through life without committing sin. Most of us sin in some way every day. In order to be saved, we must constantly beg for God's forgiveness.

And God's forgiveness is based upon the manner in which we forgive those who sin against us! If we do not forgive others, then God will not forgive us. It is just as plain as the teaching that those who are not baptized will not be saved. We stress one so loudly and so frequently. We cannot understand why some cannot accept such a plain and simple command. But somehow the matter of forgiveness gets swept under the carpet. We may sweep it under, but God will pull it out on the day of judgment and hold it up to us. Then we will have to give an answer that will be a determining factor in our eternal destiny.

> *"He who cannot forgive breaks the bridge over which he himself must pass."*

> —*George Herbert*

CLARITY OF THE SCRIPTURES

The wise writer of the book of Proverbs recognized the importance of forgiveness.

(1) "The discretion of a man deferreth his anger; and it is his glory to pass over a transgression" (Proverbs 19:11).

(2) "Rejoice not when thine enemy falleth, and let not thine heart be glad when he stumbleth" (Proverbs 24:17).

(3) "If thine enemy be hungry, give him bread to eat; and if he be thirsty, give him water to drink: for thou shalt heap coals of fire upon his head, and the Lord shall reward thee" (Proverbs 25:21,22). Note that this same thought is taught again in Romans 12:20,21.

The New Testament continues the teaching.

(1) "Blessed are the merciful, for they shall obtain mercy" (Matthew 5:7).

(2) The fifth chapter of Matthew gives some commands that completely go against the grain of human nature. "Whosoever shall smite thee on thy right cheek, turn to him the other also. And if any man will sue thee at the law, and take away thy coat, let him have thy cloak also. And whosoever shall compel thee to go a mile, go with him twain . . . Ye have heard that it hath been said, Thou shalt love thy neighbor, and hate thine enemy. But I say unto you, Love your enemies, bless them that curse you, do good to them that hate you, and pray for them which despitefully use you, and persecute you" (verses 38-44). Note that verses 45-48 continue this same line of thought.

(3) When Peter asked Christ how often must a brother be forgiven, he thought that he was being magnanimous when he suggested seven times. Imagine his surprise when Jesus answered with 490 times (Matthew 18:21,22)!

(4) When we stand praying, we should forgive others before we can expect God to forgive us (Mark 11:25).

(5) In the 35th verse of the sixth chapter of Luke, we are commanded to love our enemies and be merciful.

(6) The parable of the unmerciful servant in Matthew 18:23-35 teaches the child of God his responsibilities in forgiving others if he expects forgiveness.

(7) Paul, one of the chiefest of sinners, was very staunch in his inspired teaching:
   (a) "Being reviled, we bless; being persecuted, we suffer it: being defamed, we entreat" (1 Corinthians 4:12).
   (b) "Be ye kind one to another, tenderhearted, forgiving one another, even as God for Christ's sake hath forgiven you" (Ephesians 4:32).
   (c) "Forbearing one another, and forgiving one another, if any man have a quarrel against any: even as Christ forgave you, so also do ye" (Colossians 3:13).

(8) Other New Testament writers affirm the same teaching:

(a) "Not rendering evil for evil, or railing for railing: but contrariwise blessing" (1 Peter 3:9).

(b) "He that saith he is in the light, and hateth his brother, is in darkness even until now . . . But he that hateth his brother is in darkness, and knoweth not whither he goeth, because that darkness hath blinded his eyes" (1 John 2:9,11).

EXAMPLES

Not only do the Scriptures give direct commands—they are filled with flesh-and-blood examples of these principles personified.

(1) Esau forgave Jacob (Genesis 33:4,11).

(2) Joseph forgave his brethren (Genesis 45:5-15).

(3) Moses forgave Miriam and Aaron (Numbers 12:1-13).

(4) David forgave Saul (1 Samuel 24:10-12; 26:9,23; 2 Samuel 1:14-17).

(5) Solomon forgave Adonijah, his half-brother (1 Kings 1:5-53).

(6) Jesus forgave His enemies (Luke 23:34).

(7) In addition to the examples noted above, also consider the forgiveness received by Peter, Paul, Zacchaeus, the woman taken in adultery, and the Samaritan woman at the well.

DIFFICULTY

In view of the numerous commands just cited and all the personal examples of forgiveness noted, why is it so difficult for people to forgive one another, especially brethren?

I have given much thought to this question. After considering the pros and cons of many explanations, I believe I have reached a conclusion.

The need for forgiveness arises when an individual suffers some great emotional hurt. The one who has offended me has wounded my ego—that inner core that will fight for survival. It is a fairly simple matter to give mental assent to all the Scriptural notations mentioned earlier in this lesson. When the **emotional** me—the **real** me—is under attack, it is difficult for the intellect to rule. The same basic instinct that pushes a drowning person up for a gasp of air will also prompt anyone to try to guard his basic core of being from attack. Such a natural instinct has to be overruled by a God-trained intellect.

GREATEST HURT

Aside from a knowledge of the stark reality that those who do not forgive will themselves not be forgiven eternally, perhaps the greatest common sense motivation is simply this fact: **The one who is hurt and holds a grudge suffers more in this life than the offender.** "I will not permit any man to narrow and degrade my soul by making me hate him" (Booker T. Washington).

Just as a pretty glaze covers a common clay pot, so do flattering words hide a wicked heart. Being unforgiving and holding grudges poisons the emotions of anyone. Bitterness in the New Testament comes from the Greek word *pic*, which simply means **to cut, to prick**. It is **we** who are emotionally cut or pricked. Hebrews 12:15 speaks of the **root of bitterness**. The root may be hidden from sight, but the fruit that it produces is filled with poison. It may be manifested in a bitter tongue, prejudice and a persecution complex. In fact, chronic smoldering can be more dangerous than a cancer. Cancer can kill the body, but an unforgiving spirit can cause the soul to be lost eternally. "Water does not remain on the mountain, or vengeance in a great mind" (Oriental proverb).

When we hate someone, we become his slave. He controls our thoughts and causes stress in the body as we literally become fatigued. The person whom we hate may be miles away, but **he** is the slave driver. Bitterness becomes a boomerang as we find ourselves the recipients of the hurt.

Some act. Others react. Like an echo, they allow others to set the tone.

If one is really honest, he will have to admit that usually the person who cannot forgive others cannot forgive himself. Something deep within must first be cleansed if forgiveness can be freely offered.

MY OBLIGATIONS

After carefully studying the Scriptures mentioned earlier in this lesson, no one can deny that forgiveness is mandatory. Even common sense teaches that it is better for anyone's emotional system. In the event of a disagreement, which party bears the obligation of going to the other one in an effort to make amends?

A faithful Christian—one who is honestly trying to do what is right—bears a great responsibility. It is his task to take the initiative in making the first step where sin is involved. He certainly should be honest enough to admit his own wrong and ask for forgiveness whenever he has sinned against another. When he is innocent and someone has sinned against him, again he will take the initiative if the offender does nothing.

Look at two passages:

(1) "Moreover if thy brother shall trespass against thee, go and tell him his fault between thee and him alone: if he shall hear thee, thou hast gained thy brother" (Matthew 18:15).

(2) "Take heed to yourselves: if thy brother trespass against thee, rebuke him; and if he repent, forgive him. And if he trespass against thee seven times in a day, and seven times in a day turn again to thee, saying, I repent; thou shalt forgive him" (Luke 17:3,4).

The Scriptures clearly teach that if anyone has **sinned** against **us**, it is our Christian duty to help the person see the error of his ways or else he will be lost.

Note that the two passages mentioned above refer to **actual sin**. There is a difference between this and someone who merely "rubs us the wrong way." Sometimes he is just too blunt. Perhaps he has a gruff personality. Maybe he had a disagreement with his wife that morning and, due to irritated feelings, spoke rather sharply. He may not have any idea that he has hurt our feelings. It could be that we were overly sensitive and easily offended. Perhaps we have acquired the habit of walking around with a two-by-four piece of lumber on our shoulder instead of a mere chip. There is a difference between having our feelings hurt and having someone **sin** against us. Some people would do nothing all day long but go tell others that what they had said irritated them.

In summary, there is a difference between a brother who has sinned against us (he will die condemned) and a brother who simply said something that inadvertently hurt our feelings.

If someone has actually sinned against **us**, **we** have the obligation to go to him concerning the wrong lest he be lost eternally.

If **we** have sinned against anyone, then we have the command to go to that person and rectify the matter immediately. Matthew 5:23 reads, "Therefore if thou bring thy gift to the altar, and there rememberest that thy brother hath aught against thee; leave there thy gift before the altar, and go thy way; first be reconciled to thy brother, and then come and offer thy gift." I believe that the key lies in the previous verse. If anyone is angry with his brother without a cause or has said "Raca" (stupid one, senseless one), he is in danger of the council (Sanhedrin, who had the power to stone one to death). If he had called anyone a fool, then he would not only be in danger of losing his physical life but his soul eternally as well. In summary of this passage, if **we** go to the altar to worship and remember that **we have sinned** against our brother (in the manner described in verse 22), then **we** should delay our worship until we have gone to this brother and made the matter right.

Most of the time, when we use the term **offended**, we usually mean that our feelings have been hurt. In 1 Corinthians 8:13, the phrase "to offend" means "to sin"— "Wherefore if meat make my brother to offend, I will eat no flesh while the world standeth, lest I make my brother to offend."

In other words, if someone has merely hurt our feelings (whether willfully or unknowingly), we are not told to go "jump all over him." In maturity, we need to understand the circumstances and perhaps not even mention the incident. If, however, our brother has **sinned** against us, it is our duty to go to him lest he be lost eternally. If **we** have **sinned** against our brother (he has aught against us), then it is our duty to ask his forgiveness and make the matter right.

The Scriptures clearly teach that whether **we** have **sinned** against someone or another person has **sinned** against **us**, then **we** have the responsibility to settle the matter. I have learned not to second-guess God; but such a command assures that the grievance should be forgiven, no matter whose fault it might be. "By long forbearing is a prince persuaded, and a soft tongue breaketh the bone" (Proverbs 25:15).

WATCH THE ATTITUDE

Forgiveness is a command and must be obeyed if the child of God hopes to himself receive forgiveness from the loving Father. In dispensing our forgiveness, however, sometimes we are much like a king extending his royal scepter to anyone who will bow down and humbly ask for pardon.

In doing research for this study, I ran across these quotations:

> *"Doing an injury puts you below your enemy . . . revenging one makes you even with him . . . forgiving sets you above him."*
>
> —*Benjamin Franklin*

> *"We are like beasts when we kill. We are like men when we judge. We are like God when we forgive."*

> *"In taking revenge a man is but even with his enemy; but in passing it over, he is superior; for it is a prince's part to pardon."*
>
> —*Lord Bacon*

> *"To err is human; to forgive, divine."*
>
> —*Pope*

The quotations sounded good, and I made note of them. As I studied more and more upon this subject, I realized that the thought behind these is wrong.

Too many of us often feel that we have done a magnanimous thing in forgiving another. We actually feel superior because we are the victors. We are the ones who have risen above natural human impulses and have done something gracious. We are good. We are godly. In God's providence, we may be toppled from such a mighty attitude by experiencing a situation similar to the one mentioned in the next section.

BUT WHAT IF WE CAN'T?

"We need not put a marker on the grave when we forget a wrong and bury the hatchet."

How correct is the saying, "It is easier to forgive than forget." What a true grasp of the situation Henry Ward Beecher had when he penned, "Forgiveness ought to be like a canceled note—torn in two, and burned up, so that it never can be shown against one."

Suppose a Christian genuinely wants to forgive someone who has hurt him deeply. If the offender has actually sinned, then the child of God bears the responsibility to go to that person in order that the sin might be forgiven in God's sight. However, quite often no real sin has been committed. We may have been hurt by something that the other person is completely unaware of. We know that we should be mature enough to understand the person and the circumstances which prompted the incident and forget the matter, but the hurt lingers long after we have intellectually forgiven him. Sometimes it is even more difficult to forgive when the slight has been directed against someone whom we love dearly. We have intellectually forgiven long ago, but the feeling is not as clean as we would like for it to be. We may pray over and over, "Father, please help me not only to forgive this irritation but also to have the proper feeling toward the person." If we are truly sincere and pray long enough, then the loving Father could very well answer our prayers in a manner for which we are totally unprepared. In His providential care, He may answer that prayer by allowing us to stand in the same shoes, in a similar set of circumstances experienced by the one who has hurt us. Then we may find ourselves acting in an identical manner as our brother. When we stand in his shoes and feel the same frustrations which he must have felt, then we could very well find ourselves reacting with the same irritating response.

I know, because I have stood in those very shoes.

SUGGESTIONS FOR CLASS DISCUSSION

(1) Do you agree or disagree with the statement that one of the greatest problems facing the Church today is the inability of Christians to forgive one another? State your reasons.

(2) According to Matthew 6:12-15, the forgiveness of our own sins depends upon what?

(3) Is Mark 16:16 any more important in a person's salvation than Matthew 6:12-15? Why do you suppose we do more teaching concerning the passage in Mark?

(4) What conclusion does one reach after reading Romans 3:10, Romans 3:23, 1 John 1:8-10 and James 3:2?

(5) Why is it ever a person's glory to pass over a transgression (Proverbs 19:11)?

(6) What is the meaning of the phrase "for thou shalt heap coals of fire upon his head" found in Proverbs 25:22?

(7) Read Matthew 5:38-48. Count the number of admonitions that are contrary to human nature. Why are they so difficult?

(8) In Matthew 18:21, Peter was told that he must be willing to forgive his brother 490 times. What happens when the brother trespasses 491 times?

(9) According to Mark 11:25, we cannot pray for God's forgiveness of our wrongs until we first do what?

(10) In Luke 6:35, how are we supposed to treat our enemies? How is this possible?

(11) Relate the parable of the unmerciful servant in your own words (Matthew 18:23-35).

(12) How did Paul instruct Christians to treat one another (1 Corinthians 4:12; Ephesians 4:32; Colossians 3:13)?

(13) Examine the teachings of Peter and John on this subject (1 Peter 3:9; 1 John 2:9,11).

(14) Assign different members of the class to relate the incidents involving forgiveness on the part of Esau, Joseph, Moses, David, Solomon and Jesus. Also discuss the forgiveness received by Peter, Paul, Zacchaeus, the woman taken in adultery and the Samaritan woman at the well.

(15) Why do you think there is such difficulty in forgiving one another?

(16) Which person receives the greatest emotional hurt—the offender or the offended? Why?

(17) What is the meaning of the Greek word for bitterness? What are some fruits of bitterness?

(18) How do we become slaves to those whom we dislike so intently?

(19) Read Matthew 18:15 and Luke 17:3,4 aloud. Comment on the commands concerning the forgiveness of those who have sinned against us.

(20) Sometimes we do not use the word "offend" in the Biblical sense of sin. What is our obligation toward someone who has actually committed sin against us? What is our obligation toward a person who has irritated us or "rubbed us the wrong way"?

(21) In Matthew 5:23, which person has committed the wrong—the one who is making a sacrificial offering or the other brother?

(22) Give your own practical experiences with the teaching of Proverbs 25:15.

(23) If a Christian forgives with a condescending attitude, is he right?

(24) If we honestly want to forgive someone but can't quite seem to make our emotions do as the intellect dictates, what could the solution possibly be?

Chapter 9
GONE—
GOING—
COMING

To say that the present moment is the only important one is comparable to suddenly awakening in the air terminal without any awareness of where one has come from or any concept of one's destination.

Our lifeline is a moving line from the past to the future. We are never standing still. The writer of Ecclesiastes tells us that there is a time to be born and a time to die. The interval between the two is of deepest importance.

Each of us is a composite person. There is no line of distinction between the past, the present and the future. The roots of each phase of our lives are intertwined throughout our being. We **are** the past, the present and the future.

YESTERDAY

Many advise us to ignore the past.

> *"Finish every day and be done with it. You have done what you could. Some blunders and absurdities no doubt crept in; forget them as soon as you can. Tomorrow is a new day; begin it well and serenely and with too high a spirit to be cumbered with your old nonsense. This day is all that is good and fair. It is too dear, with its hopes and invitations, to waste a moment on yesterdays."*
>
> —Ralph Waldo Emerson

103

"No hand can make the clock strike for me the hours that are passed."

—Byron

"What's gone and past help should be past grief."

—Shakespeare

"My soul is sailing through the sea, but the past is heavy and hinders me."

—Sidney Lanier

Yet the past holds the **key** to the **present** and the **future**. It gives character and meaning to our present deeds. "The meditation of my heart shall be understanding" (Psalm 49:3).

The past can be both bitter and sweet. "Study the past if you would divine the future" (Confucius). "Commune with your own heart upon your bed, and be still" (Psalm 4:4).

Yet we should not look back unless it is to learn useful lessons from previous experiences and profit from them. The past is truly the chrysalis of today.

It has been said that the past is the sepulture of our dead emotions, but that is not true. Emotions may be buried deeply, but they never die. They must be pulled from the past, examined from an adult's standpoint and put in their proper perspective.

"The true past departs not; no truth or goodness realized by man ever dies, or can die; but all is still here, and recognized or not, lives and works through endless changes."

—Carlyle

The recalling of one thought, no matter how insignificant it may seem, can open the floodgates for a thousand memories. "Lulled in the countless chambers of the brain, our thoughts are linked by many a hidden chain; awaken but one, and lo, what myriads rise" (Pope).

Heredity (from generations past) and previous environments work hand in hand in developing the composite person we are today.

If we are to live in the present and look toward the future, yesterday has to be put in the past. However, this cannot be done until we realize how much the past influences the person we are right now. To fail to understand this fundamental principle can be a pitfall in living today victoriously.

It is good for all of us to take an objective look at the past. "Look unto the rock whence you are hewn, and to the hole of the pit from which you are digged" (Isaiah 51:1). Whether we admit it or not, the past shapes and colors each moment of today. It requires adult understanding to put previous experiences in their proper perspective.

The child is indeed the father of the man. Fortunate is the child whose early years were filled with love, security and emotional warmth. However, psychological studies show that childhood is seldom a happy experience. There is a hidden child deep inside each of us. That child's feelings never die. They may lie hidden for decades until a single word or incident can call them forth as fresh as the time of their beginning. Until that child was five or six years old, he filtered the world (the world of parents, siblings, other adults and all the external influences) through a child's mind. Some things were accepted in the subconscious mind as true without reasoning simply because they were dictated by the parents or parent figures. What seemed right was accepted. That which was ugly and hurtful was rejected or rebelled against. The events of childhood are in the past, but the hurts remain in the present.

(1) The adult feels rejection by people in general. An earlier rejection by his peers caused him to build a protective shell around his personality to guard from further rejection. The adult is seen as aloof, distant and unfriendly. More than anything else, he desires the friendship of others, but the early shield which he defensively built around himself hindered normal social interaction, and he never learned what to do to cause others to like him.

(2) The adult instinctively fears marriage because what he saw in the marriage of his parents was interpreted as hurt and disappointment. That child locked inside may later cause marital trouble.

(3) The child felt rejected by a parent. His quest for love and acceptance may be the motivating force behind a tremendous drive for acceptance in the adult.

(4) The child either witnessed rage in a parent or was a recipient of such behavior. The repulsiveness may inhibit a normal display of anger in adult life. Unreleased anger, especially over a period of time, can cause much bitterness. On the other hand, the child may follow in the steps of his parent and exhibit the same repulsive trait.

(5) A child feels inferior and inadequate to do anything correctly. The adult reaction may either be complete withdrawal or arrogant boastfulness, or the feeling may be used constructively to prod the individual to develop other talents as compensation.

(6) The child may be made to feel guilty over many things by the parent. As an adult, he cannot seem to overcome the sense of guilt and accept the grace of God. The result is chronic anxiety.

(7) Adult depression usually stems from anger turned inward. The anger may be conscious or subconscious, but its consequences can be devastating.

The usefulness of the past is immeasurable. Just as every thread of gold is priceless, so is every moment of time. To deny past feelings simply nurses them and accelerates their growth until they contaminate our entire outlook on life.

As an adult, we must call forth some feelings from the past, examine them from an adult Christian perspective, sift through the early emotions, understand their origin and glean the lessons learned. The wound must be cleaned before it can heal. Then the past can be a friend, enabling us to move from paralysis to freedom.

Happiness is not freedom from frustration—it is the ability to work through frustrations.

YOUR INNER SELF

I am the result of all that you have done and thought and felt. When you hated, that hate became a part of you. When you shirked your task, that shirking became part of you. When you lusted, that unholiness became a part of you.

*When you loved and hoped, those graces entered
into your inner self. When you chose the generous
and unselfish path, that self-forgetfulness entered
into your inner self.*

*I am the inner destiny that decided what all else
is to mean to you. When friendships are offered
you; when books invite you; when pictures allure
you; when tasks challenge you; when the future
commands you—these become either dead or full
of meaning and beauty according to what I have
become.*

*I am the sum total of your past added to the new
impulses and acts of the present. I am the final
executive officer who settles all the disputed questions of your day-to-day conduct.*

I am your inner self.

—*Author Unknown*

FUTURE

More time has been devoted to the past in this study because it seems to have a greater influence on our lives than the present or the future, yet all three are intertwined.

Actually, the future is only a wisp. There is no promise. The Scriptures teach this principle over and over.

(1) "Boast not thyself of tomorrow; for thou knowest not what a day may bring forth" (Proverbs 27:1).

(2) "Go to now, ye that say, Today or tomorrow we will go into such a city, and continue there a year, and buy and sell, and get gain: Whereas ye know not what shall be on the morrow. For what is your life? It is even a vapor, that appeareth for a little time, and then vanisheth away" (James 4:13,14).

(3) "Take therefore no thought for the morrow: for the morrow shall take thought for the things of itself. Sufficient unto the day is the evil thereof" (Matthew 6:34).

Yet tomorrow influences today.

Our hopes, goals and aspirations act as beacons, leading our paths to them. Their power is immeasurable.

On the other hand, our fears and dreads also play a significant part in the shaping of our tomorrows as well as our todays.

The kind of person we plan to be twenty years from now influences the person we are today.

PRESENT

Numerous Scriptures stress the importance of today.

(1) "Give us **this day** our daily bread" (Matthew 6:11). Note that God only gave the manna in the wilderness on a day-to-day basis.

(2) Christ taught a fundamental truth using common grass: "Wherefore, if God so clothe the grass of the field, which today is, and tomorrow is cast into the oven, shall he not much more clothe you, O ye of little faith?" (Matthew 6:30).

Some of the most significant Bible characters had pasts which had to be put into proper perspective. Often their failures spurned them on to greater service.

(1) Consider the mistake of Abraham when his life was endangered by Pharaoh in the incident of the ruler's desire to have Sarah (Genesis 12:10-20).

(2) When Moses killed the Egyptian who was smiting one of the Hebrew children, this act made it necessary for the young man who was prominent in Pharaoh's court to flee the land (Exodus 2:11-15). This sin which caused such a dramatic change in the life of Pharaoh's favored youth could have been the ruin of Moses. Evidently, he must have been able to put the wrong into its proper perspective and eventually rise to even greater heights.

(3) One has only to thumb through the pages of inspired writing to note the numerous wrongs committed by David. Although David sinned, his heart was right because he sincerely wanted to please Jehovah. This mighty ruler was always penitent when he realized his wrongs. David would never have been able to face the present unless he had first

learned to slip the past into its proper perspective.

(4) Paul considered himself to be the chiefest of sinners (1 Timothy 1:15). The manner in which he had persecuted the Christians must have weighed heavily upon his mind as he set out to convert the Gentile world. His first judgment of John Mark was in error (Acts 15:37-41), and he later admitted that this useful convert was right (2 Timothy 4:11-13).In spite of Paul's mistakes, just look at the good that this sinner did in God's service. He did not allow his past to hinder him. Instead, he used the stepping stones of mistakes to enable him to rise to heights yet unknown. Paul's philosophy is best summarized in Philippians 3:13,14: "Forgetting those things which are behind, and reaching forth unto those things which are before, I press toward the mark for the prize of the high calling of God in Christ Jesus."

No Christian can go through life looking backward. According to 2 Corinthians 5:17-19, we become new creatures. Once the infection of the past has been cleansed and the future has been understood, we must put our hand to the plow and not look back.

CONCLUSION

Once the three dimensions of time are understood, life can be victorious. It can neither be lived looking through a rearview mirror nor through binoculars.

I shall grow old, but never lose life's zest
Because the road's last turn will be the best.
—Henry Van Dyke

Grow old along with me!
The best is yet to be.
—Robert Browning

109

Look to this day!
For it is life, the very life of life.
In its brief course lie all the
Verities and realities of your existence:
For yesterday is but a dream.
And tomorrow is only a vision:
But today well lived makes
Every yesterday a dream of happiness,
And every tomorrow a vision of hope.
Look well therefore to this day!

—From the **Sanskrit**
"Salutation to the Dawn"

SUGGESTIONS FOR CLASS DISCUSSION

(1) How can each of us be a composite person of the past, present and future?

(2) Comment on the philosophy expressed by Ralph Waldo Emerson. Do you agree or disagree with it?

(3) How can the past hold the key to the present and the future?

(4) From your own experience, would you say that the past is both bitter and sweet? If you would like, share some personal examples.

(5) It is wrong to dwell in the past. When we look back, what should be the reason?

(6) Do you agree or disagree with the statement that emotions never die? Should they be ignored? What is the mature manner in which to deal with them?

(7) Have you ever happened to recall an incident that occurred many years ago? Did the feelings surrounding that incident seem just as vivid as the day they were first formed? How do you account for this?

(8) How can heredity shape the person we are today? What about the environment of earlier years?

(9) Note the passage from Isaiah 51:1.

(10) How is the child the father of the man?

(11) Discuss each of the seven examples of the manner in which childhood experiences affect the life of the adult. Add others of your own.

(12) It has been said that the wound must be cleaned before it can heal. What is the significance of this statement in view of the early experiences in our lives? What about the present hurts?

(13) Is happiness freedom from frustration? Why?

(14) Read aloud in class the selection entitled "Your Inner Self." Solicit responses from the class.

(15) Which is usually the most significant phase of time—the past, the present, or the future?

(16) Discuss the meanings of the following passages: Proverbs 27:1; James 4:13,14; Matthew 6:34.

(17) How do our hopes, goals and aspirations influence today? What powers do our fears and dreads have upon our lives?

(18) What sort of person do you plan to be twenty years from today? How does this dream affect your daily living?

(19) Why are we to only ask God for our daily bread? Does this exclude normal planning for the future?

(20) Comment on the truth taught in Matthew 6:30.

(21) Discuss some negative incidents in the lives of each of these Bible characters: Abraham, Moses, David and Paul. Add other examples. Did they become mired down in their past mistakes?

(22) Discuss Paul's philosophy in Philippians 3:13,14.

(23) Do you agree or disagree with the statement that life can neither be lived looking through a rear-view mirror nor through binoculars?

Chapter 10

RISING AGAINST THE WIND

Kim is on her way to a dental appointment when she suddenly finds herself stalled for fifteen minutes at a railroad crossing. Her muscles tighten.

Bob discovers that his position has been terminated and he no longer has a job. His hands begin to shake.

Just as Jane is ready to leave for Bible study, the baby spills milk all over his clean outfit. Jane's head begins to pound as she puts him in the bathtub while the other children run wild in their clean outfits.

Ann's mother-in-law slyly rebukes her for the manner in which she keeps house. Ann says nothing, but there is a burning within her stomach.

John and his family have just moved into town. Relatives, friends and familiar surroundings have been left behind. There is a lonely sense of not belonging.

Jean has just returned from the cemetery where her husband was laid to rest. The emptiness is overwhelming.

Sue has her hands full with the care of four preschool children. While caring for all their physical needs, she finds time for a Bible story with them each day in addition to taking them with her to all the services of the Church. Throughout the day, she tries to instill the moral principles found in their Bible studies. However, the sermon on soul-winning this morning caused her to have a very guilty feeling because she was not presently engaged in a home Bible study with an unbeliever.

All the cases cited above are suffering from a common condition affecting a majority of people in this country. In fact, most of the cases of suicide (nearly three per hour) are related to some form of this malady. It is called **stress**.

WHAT IS STRESS?

The definitions of "stress" vary. Its origin comes from the Latin word *strictus* which means "to be drawn tight." Anxiety is a synonym. So is tension. Very simply stated, stress is what we experience when we are challenged to adapt or perform.

In the March, 1978 issue of *Psychology Today,* we learn that the term "stress" was invented by Dr. Hans Selye, head of the International Institute of Stress at the University of Montreal. He states that "stress is the body's non-specific response to any demand placed on it, whether that demand is pleasant or not." Another definition is "what we experience when we are challenged to adapt or perform."

Stress may come from within or without. What is stressful to one person is not to another. **Everyone** who is alive feels stress at one time or another.

TYPES OF STRESS

Hyperstress is too much stress, as is evidenced in a racehorse. **Hypostress** is not enough stress; this is seen in a turtle.

Quite frankly, no one wants to be either a racehorse or a turtle. There has to be a happy middle ground.

If the string on a violin is too taut, it snaps. If it is too slack, it won't make music.

Destructive stress can produce both emotional and physical poisons that harm the body and emotions. Good stress can prod us to work something out; it gives us a purpose.

Let's examine each type more closely.

Eustress. Dr. Hans Selye, who was mentioned earlier, calls the challenge of turning stress into something good

114

eustress. *Eu* is the Greek word for "good." An example of eustress would be getting a top honor at school, or even the birth of a baby to a young couple. Both are good, but they evoke an excited state of emotions. Some forms of stress may not seem quite so pleasant, yet they are positive because they are for our betterment. For example, fear of fire may well be the key to preventing a child from playing with matches. The horror of an automobile accident can provide the incentive for buckling seat belts. If the stress is short in duration, and if it prods us toward a better character or a noble action, then it is eustress. It can be a test of strength of character just as the elasticity of metal is tested.

Distress. While eustress, especially when the duration is short, is good for all of us, **distress** can be very destructive.

Distress originates in the same manner as eustress. Some sort of stimulus arouses the sympathetic nervous system. Blood is pulled from the extremities back to the interior organs to provide extra energy to escape whatever danger happens to be threatening. Glandular activity accelerates. The heart races. Pupils of the eyes dilate. There is a general state of anxiety. Such emergency measures are fine if one happens to find himself in the path of a rattlesnake. But when some completely inappropriate stimulus activates such a reaction and continues for an indefinite period of time, the longevity can be devastating. Chronic fatigue, burnout, apathy and numerous psychosomatic illnesses will inevitably result.

Worry comes from the old Anglo-Saxon verb *wyrgan* and simply means "to choke." There is a free-floating anxiety that can't be pinned down. We don't know why we feel as we do. The neurotic person sees problems and dangers when they exist only in the mind, yet they produce real physical problems as happiness and productivity are destroyed.

Psychosomatic problems underlie many heart attacks, high blood pressure, strokes, migraine headaches, peptic ulcers, excessive appetite or lack of appetite, grouchiness, irritability, skin eruptions, tensions, and a general state of apprehension with no apparent cause. Dr. Charles Mayo, founder of the Mayo Clinic, observed: "Worry affects the circulation, the heart, the glands and the whole nervous system."

A person suffering from distress, or stress as it is usually called, is often a compulsive worker. He needs to produce, to

115

succeed, to be busy, to compensate, to top all other records, to atone for wrong. He feels like running most of his life, can never sit still and rest, and will not delegate authority. The early childhood tape that constantly plays inside produces feelings of guilt. His busyness resembles that of a squirrel in a cage. He fails to have positive relationships with others.

One must deal with the source rather than the symptoms. Like physical pain, it indicates that something is wrong. Most of us try to correct physical ailments and they disappear. Few, however, stop long enough to analyze and do something about the causes of stress.

If we willfully allow anything to harm our physical bodies, then we have done wrong (1 Corinthians 6:19,20).

CAUSES AND SOLUTIONS

The causes of stress are myriad. In some instances, it can be traced to one source. In others, it has multiple reasons.

(1) **Sometimes one is born with an inherited over-active central nervous system or else it is heightened early in life.** A loud tape from childhood that is constantly replayed will develop responses that are called "neurotic." Such a person cannot handle stress well. He has trouble expressing hostility and other emotions. Anger is frequently disguised by a saccharine-sweet personality. Often a compulsive behavior pattern develops, such as abnormal fear of being late or actually being perpetually late. A woman with such a behavior pattern sometimes keeps an immaculate house. Such a person may hide his or her real personality to prevent discovery. Afraid that emotions will get out of control, he puts on a false front and may not even be aware of the problem. In fact, he may consider himself to be very calm.

The fears of the child in such a case may be locked deep within the adult. The hurt that produced the stress may be in the distant past, but the symptoms are real today. The only way to deal with a stressful

116

childhood is to go to the source and probe deeply. Some people have the maturity and objectivity to analyze their own thought processes from earliest years and are able to get such feelings out in the open so they can be dealt with in an adult manner and then be placed in their proper perspectives. Most do not have such objectivity and should have professional Christian help. The stress will not disappear until the source has been found and dealt with adequately. Paul was speaking of the perfect law of liberty as contrasted with the early days of the new dispensation when he penned, "When I was a child, I spake as a child, I understood as a child, I thought as a child: but when I became a man, I put away childish things" (1 Corinthians 13:11). However, the same principle applies to each of us in the twentieth century as we understand the place and importance of early childhood feelings in our Christian lives.

(2) **The sounds and conditions of our generation are conducive to stress.** Noise is everywhere—television, radio, stereo, dishwashers and jets. There are very few places where anyone can experience peace and calm. In addition to the sounds of our generation are the anxieties produced by several depressions, World War I, World War II, Korea and Vietnam.

While it is difficult to escape the normal loud sounds of this generation, an acknowledgement of their presence and a realization of their effect can be helpful in dealing with the problem. Each of us should learn to develop a quiet place of retreat deep within.

(3) **Another important cause of stress is change.** Changes occur every day and are simply a part of life. There are times, however, when our emotional circuits can be overloaded.

An interesting study of stress caused by change was conducted by Drs. Rhomas Holmes and Richard Rahe of the University of Washington. They listed 43 events that cause major stress. These changes ranged from the death of a spouse to the loss of material possessions and were measured in life-change units. The investigation concluded that most people cannot handle more than 300 units in a year without emotional and physical suffering. For example, the death of a spouse is classified as 100 units; divorce receives 73 units; pregnancy rates 40 units while Christmas merits 12.

Often there is little that a Christian can do to prevent inevitable changes. Sometimes it helps just to know that any person would be upset with so many changes happening within a short period of time. Such feelings are normal. It is comforting to read, "For I am the Lord, I change not" (Malachi 3:6).

(4) **Uncertainty over the future produces stress.** While no one knows what the future holds, it is reassuring to realize that 40% of the things we worry about never happen, 30% of them have to do with things in the past, 12% involve our health ("what if"), 10% are insignificant and only 8% are important enough to justify concern.

Negative imaging, or imagining all the bad things that could happen, is much like black magic. It can create the very thing that one fears. Like a magnet, it draws what we dread into our lives, paralyzing each of us and making us immobile. Job succinctly stated the principle when he voiced, "For the thing which I greatly feared is come upon me, and that which I was afraid of is come unto me" (Job 3:25).

Every Christian naturally has some anxiety over the future because it is uncertain. Long ago, Paul experienced the same feeling when he said, "And now, behold, I go bound in the spirit unto Jerusalem, not knowing the things that shall befall me there" (Acts 20:22).

Perhaps the best prescription can be found in Romans 8:28: "And we know that all things work together for good to them that love God, to them who are the called according to his purpose." God expects us to do everything within our ability to intelligently plan for the future and then leave the rest to Him because everything will eventually work together for the best for God's faithful. That one verse does wonders in reducing stress!

(5) **Conflict between people can precipitate great stress.** No one lives by himself unless he selects the life of a hermit. If we are to enjoy the benefits of companionship, then we must accept the probability of inevitable friction. The realization that it is impossible to please everyone may be of some help in dealing with stress. However, we should be honest enough to admit that a great deal of the burden could very well rest upon our own shoulders. The chapter that deals with loving others should give insight to this problem.

(6) **Criticism is a factor in producing stress.** Criticism puts us on the defensive and tears down our self-worth, especially when we try to please too many people. Sometimes the criticism is deserved and should be used beneficially to correct some defect in our own lives. There are other times, however, when the sharp words are undeserved. Then we must use good judgment in helping us decide whether we should go to that person or simply develop a thicker hide.

(7) **Fear of failure can cause tremendous stress in a person's life.** No one likes to fail. We all like to succeed. Yet common sense should tell anyone that the only person who never makes a mistake is the person who never tries. We must have a good feeling of self-worth if we can successfully fail. (Yes, that sentence was intended to be worded in that manner!) A study of the chapter dealing with the command to love ourselves would be helpful with this type of stress. "For God hath not given us the spirit of fear; but of power, and of love, and of a sound mind" (2 Timothy 1:7).

If you are a person who is overinvolved, let me urge you to sit down and probe deeply into your reasons. Be careful what you request in your prayers. Sometimes we ask for a virtue but are not quite prepared for the events sent our way to enable us to develop that trait. Remember that God is just as interested in **who** we **are** as in **what** we are

doing. When we get our priorities in order, it becomes easier to objectively sort through all our activities and have enough conviction to admit, "That may be a worthwhile task, but it is too much. I need to drop those things that do not relate to what is most important in my life." The blessings are immeasurable.

(9) **A contradiction with our set of moral values is stressful.** Most of us can carry a reasonable load as long as we feel that what we are doing is right. If there is a conflict, however, one plus one equals far too many. For example, a young Christian may find himself in a new condition away from home. There is strong peer pressure to participate in certain activities which the youth has always considered to be wrong. If the Devil succeeds in convincing him that the action in question is really not wrong, then there will probably be no stress. If he goes ahead and participates knowing that what he is doing is wrong, stress is certain to develop.

Good things that are not morally wrong can also produce stress. Allow me to give a personal example. Just a couple of years ago, I had accepted a number of invitations to speak at ladies' day seminars, workshops and other gatherings of Christian women. During that year, there were two incidents within about a month of each other that caused me to stop and realize what I was doing. Our daughter called from out of town and told me that she had planned to come home for Mother's Day but had noticed in my last letter that I was going to be speaking out of town on that particular weekend. Within a month, I had to ask my own daddy to wait and come on the Monday after Father's Day because I was going to be traveling back from a speaking engagement on that Sunday. It made me stop and think. There was a conflict in my set of values. Although the speaking was an important work in God's service, I had allowed it to crowd out my family. I canceled other engagements until I could get my priorities straightened out.

(10) **Our self-image can also produce stress.** We have all heard and read a great deal about setting high

120

goals for ourselves if we are ever to succeed in life. In fact, one entire chapter of this study is devoted to that line of thought. Few of us would ever do anything worthwhile unless we have positive reasonable goals to prod us along.

However, some carry the idea of goals and high standards a bit too far. When we expect ourselves to accomplish the impossible, we are doomed to failure and stress. No person can expect himself to be perfect. If our own self-image is that of a flawless person who is consistently performing a phenomenal number of worthwhile activities, stress is inevitable.

A mature Christian should take an objective look at himself and his own self-image in order to discern whether or not it is "reasonable" (Romans 12:1). If it is not, then he should make some changes in his thinking.

(11) **Repression of deep feelings can precipitate stress.** The thrust of this cause of stress was discussed earlier in conjunction with the effect that the early childhood years can have upon an adult's life. No emotion ever dies. Whether it comes during the first years of life or during the adult phase, negative emotions should never be repressed or suppressed. We may pack dirt on top of them, but they are still there. While it is wrong to express them in rage or in any way that will hurt someone else, they must be dealt with if we are ever to rid ourselves of the stress which they produce. An admission that they are there is the first step. An examination to discover the reasons for their existence is next in order. Both of these are futile, however, unless there is a spirit of willingness to cleanse any wrong motives. The results can be amazing.

(12) **Open sin and rebellion against God can produce the greatest stress of all.** If a person allows his conscience to become seared with a hot iron (1 Timothy 4:2), then naturally his sins will produce little stress. The normal person, however, whose heart has not become hardened will be pricked in his conscience whenever he does something that he knows is against the will of God. Actually, this is a good

kind of stress and should not be eliminated from anyone's life since it can make the difference in whether or not a person is saved or lost. It was this condition that prompted the Jews on the day of Pentecost to be pricked in their hearts and ask, "Men and brethren, what shall we do?" (Acts 2:37). This same stressful realization of sin caused the astonished and trembling Saul to ask, "Lord, what wilt thou have me to do?" (Acts 9:6).

CONCLUSION

The list of causes of stress and the accompanying suggestions for their removal is by no means exhaustive. The reader can add many more. However, there are some conclusions that are applicable to almost any form of stress.

(1) **The Scriptures repeatedly warn of the dangers of remaining in a stressful condition.** Even Jehovah realized that rest or relaxation was necessary. "And on the seventh day God ended his work which he had made: and he rested on the seventh day from all his work which he had made" (Genesis 2:2).

Moses, who carried the burden of leading thousands of people for forty years, was advised by his father-in-law, Jethro, to seek helpers. "The thing that thou doest is not good. Thou wilt surely wear away, both thou, and this people that is with thee: for this thing is too heavy for thee; thou art not able to perform it thyself alone" (Exodus 18:17,18). As a result, men were selected to judge many of the minor grievances of the people in order that Moses could concentrate upon the more important matters.

Christ is our supreme example of effectively dealing with all the pressures of life. In the midst of a throng of people who were clamoring for attention appeared Jairus, beseeching the Master's aid in healing his dying daughter. As Jesus began to follow the distraught father, more and more people thronged around him. After healing the woman who had been ill for twelve years and then raising the daughter of Jairus, the Son of God experienced the emotional torture of rejection at Nazareth, commissioned the twelve and then experienced the natural feelings of losing a close friend and relative. Very wisely He urged His apostles, "Come ye yourselves apart into a desert place, and rest a while: for there were many coming and going, and they had no leisure so much as to eat" (Mark 6:31). After that, they departed into a desert place by ship privately. Christ had a good rhythm of life. He was constantly among the people as He went about His work of healing and teaching, yet even He periodically went up into a mountain alone to pray.

The child of God can withstand a tremendous amount of external pressure as long as this outer pressure is balanced with an inner strength. If God, Christ, Moses and many more could understand that they needed times of rest and quiet, then why do we have such difficulty in comprehending?

(a) "For I have learned, in whatsoever state I am, therewith to be content" (Philippians 4:11).

(b) "Commune with your own heart upon your bed, and be still" (Psalm 4:4).

(c) "Be silent, O all flesh, before the Lord" (Zechariah 2:13).

(d) "A time to keep silence, and a time to speak" (Ecclesiastes 3:7).

To remain in a stressful condition, whatever its cause, is to willfully defile the temple of God if there is anything within our power that we can do to alleviate the problem.

(2) **One's attitude is the key.** A stressor is neutral. Our reaction to that stressor determines whether it will produce stress in our bodies or minds. Only we can control our attitudes, and there is no way that a human being can have the right attitude without God's help.

(3) **Look ahead. Plan.** Try to eliminate stressful situations. Some people thrive on the challenge of meeting deadlines; others go to pieces. Try to analyze

your own temperament. If deadlines bother you, plan ahead and don't allow them to master you.

(4) **Delegate authority.** Perhaps nothing can equal the stress which results from the feeling that no one else can do something as well as oneself. Evidently, some Christians must think that an exhausted, haggard appearance is a sign of true spirituality. "Look at all the things I must do in the work of the Church. No one else will do them. Poor me!" We would all do well to heed Jethro's advice to Moses and delegate part of the workload to others. In addition to relieving ourselves of some of the stress, we would be giving others an opportunity to develop their own spiritual muscles. When we think we have to do it all, we are much like the football player who thought he had to play all the quarters and then sell popcorn and Cokes at halftime because no one else would do it. It's rather ridiculous, isn't it?

(5) **Diversify.** Most of us can withstand many of the pressures of this life if we can only learn to diversify—to take a break in our activities. Even a change to a different kind of work can be relaxing.

(6) **Try to live one day at a time.** This is more easily said than done. The old saying "Life is hard by the yard, but by the inch it's a cinch!" is so true. "Take therefore no thought for the morrow: for the morrow shall take thought for the things of itself. Sufficient unto the day is the evil thereof" (Matthew 6:33). How true are the words of Henry Ward Beecher: "It is not work that kills men: it is worry. Work is healthy. Worry is rust upon the blade."

(7) **Realize that it is possible to be occupied with worthless leisure activities.** Constantly running from one form of recreation or relaxation can actually produce stress. We must learn to be selective even with our leisure.

(8) **Learn to relax.** Note that this admonition said **learn**. Relaxation comes easily for some. They just naturally "hang loose." For others, it is an art to be learned. Telling a person to relax and not worry is similar to telling someone with a broken leg not to

limp. It is more easily said than done.

There is an old saying that wisely advises, "You will break the bow if you keep it always bent." The body can be taught certain physical relaxation procedures. Relaxing is a learned reflex. Tight muscles must be conditioned to "let go." It is time well spent.

Just as the body must often be taught to relax, so must the mind. However, it is more difficult to train a mind to relax than a body. Usually a busy, tense person seldom relinquishes time for relaxation. In order to get in the habit, it may be necessary to make appointments with oneself for rest. Even though the body may be unable to be in restful surroundings, with some trained imagination the mind can take mini-vacations several times each day. Silence truly is golden. "Never is one more active than when he does nothing; never is he less alone than when he is by himself" (Cato).

The victorious Christian is one who has learned to rise above the normal stress of this world. He can voice the words of John Greenleaf Whittier:

> *Drop Thy still dews of quietness*
> *Til all our strivings cease;*
> *Take from our souls the strain and stress*
> *And let our ordered lives confess*
> *The beauty of Thy peace.*

SUGGESTIONS FOR CLASS DISCUSSION

(1) Give the definition of "stress" as it is presented in the lesson. Add your own comments.

(2) What is the difference between "hyperstress" and "hypostress"? Is either one desirable in humans?

(3) What is "eustress" and how is it beneficial?

(4) What is the difference between "eustress" and "distress"?

(5) "Distress" is usually referred to as "stress." What are some of the physical symptoms of stress? What happens to the body if such conditions exist for a long period of time? Relate your conclusions to 1 Corinthians 6:19,20.

(6) What are the causes of an overactive central system? Whether it is an inherited trait or one developed early in childhood, what are some of its characteristics? If a person who had a very stressful childhood lacks the emotional maturity to analyze his own behavior, whom should he consult for guidance? What are the dangers of counseling with someone who is not a Christian?

(7) How can the sounds and conditions of our generation be conducive to the development of stress?

(8) How can a normal change (one that is even good) produce stress? Discuss the findings of Drs. Holmes and Rahe.

(9) Stress can be caused by uncertainty over the future. Is this normal? How can constantly thinking about all the bad things that could happen bring them about? Discuss the prescription for fear of the future as it is found in Romans 8:28. Cite examples from your own experiences.

(10) Since conflict between people can be stressful, what are some suggestions that you have personally found to be beneficial?

(11) Have you ever had some form of criticism cause personal hurt and stress? What is the best way to handle most types of criticism?

(12) Some failure is inevitable and naturally produces stress. How can we successfully fail?

(13) Overinvolvement is stressful. What are some of the negative things in which we tend to become overinvolved? How can overinvolvement even in good things also produce a stressful condition? What does Romans 12:1 tell us about what God expects?

(14) Why is God just as interested in what we **are** as in what we are **doing**?

(15) Have you ever felt the stress that comes from a contradiction with your set of moral values? How did you handle the situation?

(16) If our goals are too high and our self-image is one of perfection, what is bound to happen? How can low expectations and a low self-image also produce stress? What is the answer?

(17) Can negative feelings ever be successfully repressed? What can we do with them and be pleasing to God?

(18) What is the most stressful condition in anyone's life? What can be done about it?

(19) How did Jehovah, Christ and Moses deal with stressful situations? What is the example for us today?

(20) Since a stressor is neutral, how is attitude the key?

(21) How can planning ahead eliminate much stress?

(22) Why do most people usually hesitate to delegate authority?

(23) Give some examples of diversification. How have they helped in your life?

(24) In a brainstorming session, compile a list of suggestions for living one day at a time. Is there a contradiction in this and intelligently planning for the future?

(25) What are some examples of worthless leisure activities?

(26) How can the body and the mind be taught to relax?

(27) Conclude the class with the hymn that contains the words of John Greenleaf Whittier.

Chapter 11
GOOD AND MAD

I suppose there has been more controversy over the control of anger than any other emotion. Most books advise a **good** quarrel now and then to promote a better relationship. Others urge the irritated party to go for a long walk, work in the yard, clean out all the drawers and closets, go out in the woods and either yell or hit something if such action promotes better feelings. Some maintain that Christians should be mature enough to totally ignore the situation and act as if there had never been any hurt feelings. Somewhere in the maze of books, articles, tapes, films and lectures, there has to be an answer. Personally, I have struggled with it for years and have only recently found what I believe to be the truth. It is based upon two premises.

(1) Understand **why** you become hurt or angry.

(2) Learn how to handle such emotions in an acceptable manner.

UNDERSTANDING WHY

Intellect. Emotions. The two are so different that each requires a separate part of the brain for its functions.

The left hemisphere of the brain is the center of the intellect—the conscious part of the mind. It primarily controls logical, analytical and rational thinking.

The right hemisphere, on the other hand, handles information sent to it in an abstract and symbolic manner. It is this part that dictates one's creative, intuitive and impulsive thought processes.

The left side reasons. The right side feels.

Any relationship between two people thrives on good feelings—love, generosity, happiness, self-confidence, a sense of worth and acceptance—but not all feelings are good. Some are hostile and produce bad actions that serve only to smother good feelings. Fear, pride, rage, selfishness, criticism, grudges, pouting, arrogance, loneliness, hate, guilt, anxiety, inferiority, frustrations, bragging, aggressiveness, aloofness—all strike at the heart of any relationship between two people with a deadly poison. Each can trace its origin to the same source—an inability to properly express emotions.

A person's intellect may dictate that he should not be selfish, angry, or spiteful. However, if the emotions feel crushed or mistreated in some way, then it is the right side of the brain that reacts with rage or even complete withdrawal. That part of the brain doesn't reason. It simply reacts.

A mature Christian should not respond to negative situations as a two-year-old youngster childishly vents his frustrations in temper tantrums. Neither should he fearfully and perhaps stoically deny his feelings. The world generally denounces the first and rewards the second, yet both can be devastating.

Emotional maturity recognizes emotions for what they are, understands their origins, and then sensibly handles them in a Christian manner. Such a statement can be read in seconds but may require months of soul-searching to accept such as the truth in one's own personal life.

A woman may scream and throw dishes at her husband in a fit of rage. He may shout hateful, cutting words as he even physically strikes her. One of them may poutingly remain silent for days while the other feverishly cleans house or the garage. Contrastingly, they both may be super-sweet to one another, even when irritated, in an effort to prevent rocking the boat or making waves. As opposite as some of these emotions may seem, they are all defensive mechanisms for one of the most basic of all human emotional needs. At the core of every person is the desire to be loved and accepted to some satisfying degree. This is just as essential for emotional

130

development as food and water are to the physical body. Every person needs to feel good about himself. He can't love others until he first loves himself (Matthew 22:39), and he can't love himself (another phrase for self-concept) until he in turn feels loved and accepted.

Practically all negative emotions can be traced to a lack of adherence to this important command of Christ. Emotions cannot be corrected in any relationship until this basic need has been understood.

Persons who seem shy and aloof may be compared to a flower that never opened. An early feeling of rejection in some form or another may have prevented such people from lovingly stretching forth their arms to others for fear of being hurt. They never felt good about themselves and have developed a lifestyle by walling others out either by aggression or withdrawal. The painfully shy person and the brash bully are both actually trying to shield themselves from further hurt or rejection. Some suppress their innermost feelings, hiding them deeply inside the subconscious part of the mind. Others even go a step further and actually repress the emotions. Repression is a denial to self because the feeling seems to be wrong or unworthy. Neither suppressed nor rejected feelings die. They will always remain deeply implanted in the subconscious mind, festering much as a splinter and closing the doors to a warm, loving relationship with anyone.

It has been observed that the four basic emotions move in different directions. In rage, one moves against whatever is producing the irritation. Fear causes movement away from the source of trouble. Depression turns the emotion inward against oneself. Love, on the other hand, moves toward the source of pleasure.

MAKING THE APPLICATION

Much has been discussed in theory. The time has come to make concrete applications.

It has been said that nothing needs to be feared—only understood. An awareness of the main causes of most of human relationship problems is essential before any corrective measures can be taken.

131

It can be stated simply. At the core of everyone is the ego or the self. "Thou shalt love thy neighbor as thyself" (Matthew 22:39). Any person will naturally defend this inner core whenever it is threatened or rejected. This reaction (the defense of an irritation) is just as natural as breathing.

For years we have sung, "Angry words, oh let them never from the tongue unbridled slip." We consider all anger as sin. Perhaps most Christians have never learned how to deal properly with this emotion. That could well be one of the causes of many divorces in Christian homes. Most of God's people don't even recognize anger when they meet it face to face. We think of it in terms of rage or wrath. Since anger is considered sinful, we justify our wounded feelings by calling them hurts, mistreatment and frustrations. These definitions make us sound like martyrs. We may suffer wrongs and others may not treat us as they should, but one day we will have our reward.

Most children of God don't realize that hurts or injustices are really feelings of anger. Some of us have denied anger so long that we fail to recognize it. We may have developed a defensive attitude that seems to be holy in the eyes of the world, but the wrong has never been recognized, dealt with and cleansed. It simply festers and pollutes from within. Anger and hurt are different words for the same feelings— irritated emotions. We are angry—intensely angry—because someone has wounded our self-esteem, our inner beings. We are not simply **hurt**—we are **angry**. Admit it! God, who most certainly felt anger on many occasions, knew the feeling and even gave rules for dealing with this emotion.

HANDLING ANGER

(1) **In Ephesians 4:26, we are commanded, "Be ye angry, and sin not."**
Call anger by its name. A certain amount of irritation is inevitable when anyone deals with other people. This irritation of the emotions is not wrong. It is a fact of life and is just as natural as eating. Having a good appetite is not wrong; neither is anger. But the manner in which each is handled can be sinful.

132

It is wrong to try to slide a hurt or slight under a rug and pretend that it is not there. It is there! It will not go away. If the feeling is blocked, it will not become non-existent. Instead, it will smoulder in the subconscious mind while the person affected behaves as if nothing ever happened. Such poison within one's system may either be blocked or can frequently be vented on an innocent person. Sometimes we turn the anger upon our own selves in the form of depression. Some sense a floating anxiety. Others deal with anger by overeating, by overworking, by talking too much or too little, by all sorts of psychosomatic illnesses, or by being critical of everyone. Some of us are so fearful of hurts that we are **overly nice** to all (even scoundrels) in a desperate attempt to be accepted and loved instead of once again having our inner beings hurt.

Yet fear of being hurt may use entirely different protective devices—wrath, physical abuse, tantrums, shouting and many other related actions. All of these are bad. All are desperate cover-up measures to protect ourselves against hurt.

In effect, God is saying, "Don't yell or scream when you are upset. But neither should you try to deny hurt feelings and pretend that they don't exist. When you are irritated over something, be mature enough to pull the emotion out into the light and call it by its right name—**anger!**"

Once we have eyeballed anger and have called the irritated emotion by its right name, then we should deal with it in a manner that is not sinful.

Thus, the first guideline for dealing with anger is to recognize the emotion and admit it to ourselves. "Be ye angry" is natural. We should admit that we are angry instead of lying to ourselves and others. In the preceding verse, the Christian is admonished, "Wherefore putting away lying, speak every man with his neighbor: for we are members one of another."

The command may be summarized very simply: **Recognize your irritated emotions for what they are—anger. Don't lie about them to yourself or to others. Dissipate them before they cause you to sin.**

(2) **"Let not the sun go down upon your wrath."**

The above command is just as binding as any other, but few of us accept it, and even fewer put it into practice. We not only count to ten, we go on up to a million. We deny. We act nice. We pretend that if we ignore the feeling, it will go away.

But it doesn't.

God commanded us to get the emotion out into the open, admit it and do something about it before the sun goes down. In other words, dissipate the emotion right away before it can do any lasting harm.

Failure to recognize an irritation and dissipate it immediately is probably one of the greatest causes of disagreement. When an emotion isn't dealt with maturely and immediately, it grows and grows. It becomes bigger and more obnoxious. When it reaches such gigantic proportions, solutions seem impossible. If only it had been nipped in the bud, much agony could have been spared.

There are at least five different ways to rid ourselves of anger. Let's examine both the advantages and disadvantages of each of them.

(a) **Talk to the one with whom we have conflict immediately.** After all, weren't God's people admonished to stop in the middle of offering their gifts upon the altar until they had first talked with the one against whom they had sinned (Matthew 5:23)? On the other hand, if our brother has actually sinned against us, we are to talk with him (Matthew 18:15; Luke 17:3,4).

Rather than have ill feelings that fester and grow into tremendous monsters deep inside our beings, we should be able to talk things over. However, very few people have had training in the techniques of venting their feelings to others in a Christian manner.

If someone has sinned against us, it is usually best to talk with that person about the problem. If **we** have sinned against another person, then we should also be willing to talk. However, this cannot happen in a Christian manner until we have established good communications. Grievances should not be told in rage. Remember that when we fly off the handle and retort with cutting remarks, we may be allowing ourselves to feel better; but, at the same time, we are attacking the self-esteem of the person who has hurt us. Our rage (or even physical demonstrations) usually causes the other person to utilize every protective measure that she or he can imagine, whether it be retaliating with his own words of wrath or by packing his own hurt deeply down inside his inner being where it festers and erupts later in a totally inappropriate manner. Most of us treat others as we **have** been treated.

Also, a person can adopt **flying off the handle** as a way of life—a problem-solving tool. This habit encourages us to lash out at every problem, regardless of the significance, as a way of life. Explosive rage thus becomes a cathartic habit, and we adopt it as a solution to every problem. No one enjoys being with such a person. He really cannot tolerate himself because of his continued aggression. He has become a victim of chronic rage.

Certainly we should have good communication which allows us to sit down and tell someone that we have been offended. We should also be able to sense whenever we have hurt someone else and can gently discuss the grievance. Whatever happened to manners? "A soft answer turneth away wrath: but grievous words stir up anger" (Proverbs 15:1).

(b) **We can get off to ourselves and yell, scream, or hit something to let off steam.** The advantage of this method is a release of pressure within us. It can be therapeutic in releasing emotions without hurting anyone. But we are someone. If such actions cause us to feel guilty or ashamed of ourselves, then our original anger will only be intensified.

(c) **Tell someone else.** Sometimes it seems best not to encounter the person who has offended us. Neither does letting off steam by ourselves seem to help. Frequently, talking to someone else about our problems can help. There are advantages in expressing our feelings aloud, especially to another person. Perhaps that person can be objective and can give needed advice. All this is good, but there are also dangers. Too often, such a one is untrustworthy and will tell others or even the one who has made us angry. Sometimes we rehearse our anger so often that it is strengthened instead of being dissipated.

Problems can be discussed with a trustworthy person in an effort to get our troubles in a proper perspective and finally rid ourselves of them. It should not be done if such a measure spreads the information or deepens the hurt within us by rehearsing it over and over.

(d) **Write the grievance down on paper.** Pray about the matter. Burn the paper. Such corrective measures have their merit. They get the bitterness out of our systems in much the same way as yelling in the middle of the forest or kicking the stump of a tree. No other person has been hurt. We have given ourselves a little time to "cool off" and see things in a proper perspective. Most importantly, we have poured our hearts out to God. He is truly our strength.

However, such measures do not help the one who has offended us to see the wrong which he has done.

(e) **Admit the feeling of anger to ourselves alone.** We don't call it hurt. We do not say that we have been mistreated. We recognize the fact that our emotions have been irritated. We are **angry**.

It is then that we can take mature Christian action. Each case is different. Sometimes, objectively viewing the irritation for what it is will cause it to seem inconsequential. It really is not important enough to even bother the one who has irritated us with the problem. The vexations may prove to be trifles when brought out in the light, especially when compared to our own shortcomings and the problems that the other person faces. However, the annoyances may bother us enough that we should use one of the above-mentioned methods of handling the problem. It does not matter how slight the irritation may be. If it annoys us enough, we should do something to dissipate the emotion until it loses its force.

In gleaning the message from Ephesians 4:25-32, we may summarize: **Admit your irritation as anger. Don't lie about it to yourself or to others. Anger is natural, but do not allow it to cause you to sin. Examine the feelings as a mature Christian and decide upon the best method to rid yourself of this emotion. Do not postpone handling the matter until tomorrow. Neither should you** use harsh, irritating methods of communicating your hurt with the one who has either wronged you or has been hurt by you. Bitterness, wrath, malice and angry words have no place in conveying your feeling to another. Dissipate it with kindness and a tender, forgiving heart before night comes.

SUGGESTIONS FOR CLASS DISCUSSION

(1) Should emotions be expressed? For example, when one is extremely annoyed over an irritation, is it better for him to throw a plate or retire to his room and refuse to speak for hours? Is either reaction a solution to the problem?

(2) Compare the functions of the left and right sides of the brain. Why do we need both?

(3) Cite examples of good feelings. Why is their expression so important in a marriage?

(4) What are some hostile feelings? What effect can they have on any relationship?

(5) What happens when hostile feelings are expressed without any restrictions? By way of contrast, what is the typical result of the denial of such emotions?

(6) Comment on this statement: The left side of the brain reasons with the **intellect** whereas the right side reacts with **feelings**.

(7) The world urges individuals to vent their emotions. "Get them out in the open even if it requires an angry rage to do so." The common belief of Christianity admonishes, "It is wrong to become angry and feel displeasure. One should be in full control of his emotions." Which is right? Could they both be wrong?

(8) How can rage, silence and super-sweetness all be ways of handling the same emotion?

(9) At the core of every person is what desire? Is it wrong?

137

(10) Study Matthew 22:35-39. Divide the class into three groups to discuss the three great loves taught here. Why is this command so important?

(11) Describe the development of some protective devices that a person commonly develops from hurts in early childhood.

(12) What is the difference between "suppressed" and "repressed" feelings? Do they ever die? How can we deal with them effectively?

(13) In what direction do these emotions move: rage, fear, depression, love?

(14) At the core of anyone is the ego, self-esteem, self-concept (all are words or phrases for the self, the real person). Why is it only natural to defend this inner part of ourselves? What effect does this have upon marriage?

(15) How can hurts or injustices be other words for anger?

(16) Christians have long been taught that anger is wrong and must be restrained. What is the difference between justifiable anger (irritated emotions, hurts, injustices) and wrath?

(17) What will happen to an irritated emotion if it is not admitted and cleansed?

(18) Examine these instances of God's anger (Exodus 4:14; Numbers 11:10,11). Since God is divine, what does His anger teach us? Use a concordance to discuss other examples of God's anger.

(19) Is it natural for two strong personalities to blend into the oneness of marriage without some irritations? Cite examples. Why do we usually become angry with someone whom we truly love?

(20) Why does Ephesians 4:26 command "Be ye angry"? Why does the same verse admonish "and sin not"? How can temper tantrums, psychosomatic illnesses, overeating, overworking, withdrawal, depression, anxiety and artificial sweetness all be ways in which we often sin when we are angry?

(21) Discuss the summary of the command in Ephesians 4:26. "Recognize your irritated emotions for what they are—anger. Don't lie about them to yourself or to others.

Dissipate them before they cause you to sin." What is your evaluation?

(22) Why are we commanded not to let the sun go down upon our wrath? Reconcile this to the theory that many hurts become inconsequential with the passing of time.

(23) The lesson suggests five different ways to rid ourselves of anger. Divide the class into five groups to discuss both the advantages and disadvantages of each.

(24) How can telling someone about a hurt or injustice help to dissipate the feeling? How can the same method be used to rehearse a grievance and cause it to become even more intense? What is the answer to the problem?

(25) Use these verses for further enrichment: Psalm 30:5; Proverbs 15:1; Proverbs 16:32; Proverbs 16:22; Proverbs 19:11; Proverbs 27:3-6; Proverbs 29:22; Psalm 37:8; Proverbs 22:24; Proverbs 30:33; Ecclesiastes 7:9; Amos 1:11; Jonah 4:4; Matthew 5:22; James 1:19; Psalm 52:2; Psalm 64:3; Psalm 120:2; Psalm 140:3; Proverbs 6:16,17; Proverbs 10:11; Proverbs 10:19; Proverbs 15:4; Proverbs 15:28; Proverbs 16:27; Proverbs 18:8; Proverbs 18:21; Proverbs 26:21; Ephesians 4:25; Ephesians 4:31.

Chapter 12
HOLDING PATTERNS

Sometimes life seems to fall apart.

We as Christians (yes, even strong, dedicated ones) may find ourselves in a position where there seems to be no progress. We feel that we are locked on dead center. There is no forward flying, no goals being reached, no mountains being scaled. There is simply a frustrating circling—**a treading of water to keep our heads up**. Progress seems to be blocked. All that we can do is wait.

CAUSES

What produces these holding patterns?

Sometimes they are caused by sin and our stubborn rebellion. There is no room for God.

At other times, such periods of life are produced by the natural circumstances of daily living. After all, a life span is filled with its ups and downs. A great deal of the time, we are able to take them in stride and can rise above the variations. At other times, we become mired in the muck of living. Not only are we unable to make any real spiritual progress, we are desperately fighting to keep from slipping backward. The very best that we can do is keep our heads above water.

(1) **The sickness of a loved one can hinder spiritual growth.** There are occasions when a critical illness

141

can actually bring one closer to God. Although such times are low points in the pattern of life, they can provide the thrust to rely completely upon God and become stronger Christians. Sometimes such an illness—as in the constant care of an invalid, especially when it goes on and on, year in and year out—can actually sap anyone's spiritual strength. There is less time and motivation for Bible study. Assembling with the saints (and drawing strength and encouragement from others) becomes irregular. There is neither the time nor ability to reach out in performing natural Christian duties. At times, we feel drained and even resentful. Feelings of guilt then inch their way into our subconscious minds. We are standing still. We feel our feet beginning to sink. We are afraid.

(2) **Our own physical illness can produce many of the problems associated with the sickness of a loved one, especially if the days drag into weeks and the weeks lengthen into years.** Few people in such a situation can evade self-pity. "All these other people are walking around living normal lives. Why does my body have to suffer so much?" A chronically ill person can actually do much to increase his own spirituality and even reach out to others in a limited way. When one is a shut-in, however, there are fewer opportunities for contact with the outside world; and self-motivation over a sustained period of time is difficult to maintain. Often there are feelings of guilt—the worry of being a bother to whoever is caring for such a one. Not feeling up to par (even though not critically ill) coupled with a lack of stimulus can produce a real holding pattern.

(3) **A conflict with a loved one or a close personal friend can freeze spiritual growth.** Such an irritation can easily short-circuit the flow of Christianity. In the first place, a Christian naturally feels guilt over the conflict. Secondly, it is difficult for a child of God to function productively when there is such a disturbance. Our emotional makeup has a natural sense of priorities. Such a conflict is an

attack on one's ego, and all physical and emotional systems naturally give preference to the priority of self-preservation. True worship and service in the kingdom are practically impossible at such a time.

(4) **Whenever a loved one is in trouble, few will make any spiritual strides.** Whether the distressed one is a mate, father, mother, child, any other family member or a friend, we are closely attached to such a person. Quite often, we feel their hurts almost as deeply as if they were our own. We feel their shame, their agony, their distress. Sometimes it seems that there are no clear-cut answers. We want to help so badly but don't know how. Of course, helping anyone in need is an integral part of Christianity. When we feel that we can assist, we rise above the situation and fly. But sometimes the answers are not so evident. We want to help but can't. We agonize. Instead of flying, we tread water. We find ourselves in a holding pattern.

(5) **The loss of a loved one inhibits spiritual growth for a time.** Sorrow and grief are only natural. It takes time to work our way through such a trauma. Feelings of resentment are only natural. "Why did my loved one have to be taken away from me?" The grieved one may not voice the sentiment, but often the emotion is actually that of anger. The sooner the one left behind can get a grip on the innermost feelings and bring them out into the open, the more quickly the problem can be resolved. Emotions never die. They either smoulder and grow more intense or else they are brought to light, acknowledged and handled in a mature, Christian manner. Grief has its natural stages, and one must work his way through each one. Such a situation turns one's thoughts inward, and it is extremely difficult to make spiritual strides.

(6) **The trauma of a move to a new location and the establishing of a new circle of friends can often take precedence over a proper spiritual relationship with God.** Everyone needs friends. All have a basic need to feel accepted and wanted. These needs of the emotional system are just as

vital as food and water are to the physical system. The most compelling thoughts of a starving person are seldom spiritual. Of utmost importance are ways in which such physical necessities can be obtained. Any troubled person should turn to God for strength, but human nature usually looks first to the fulfillment of basic needs, and friendship is one of those needs.

(7) **The loss of a job or material possessions can cause spiritual stagnation.** A Christian may be doing tremendous work in the Church—faithful attendance, teaching, reaching lost souls, and participation in every phase of the work. Suddenly there is no income. Perhaps there is a massive job layoff. Maybe one's own business fails. A devastating fire could wipe out a house and all other material goods. The feeling is one of bewilderment. Fear. Panic. Where will I get the money to pay the utilities? How can we buy next week's groceries? Our home will be repossessed if we do not make the monthly payments. There will be no car to even drive to the worship services. In the event of a fire, where will I sleep tonight? Next week? What will I wear? On and on the worries mount. The economic recession during recent years has placed more and more middle or upper middle income families in such a predicament. Normally faithful Christians are finding their thoughts turned toward pressing financial worries rather than the urgency of teaching lost souls. Until living can once again be stabilized, most Christians who are faced with such a crisis find themselves in a holding pattern rather than flying straight toward a spiritual goal.

(8) Although it may seem paradoxical after considering the reason for the holding pattern discussed in the previous section, **a lack of financial or material problems can lull us into a sense of false security and precipitate spiritual stagnation.** We feel completely self-reliant. We have worked hard and are enjoying the fruits of our labors. We feel that we deserve what we have. We have worked. We have planned. We have sacrificed.

144

Somewhere along the line, we have developed the attitude that we do not need God. We are not becoming stronger and better Christians. We are circling in a holding pattern.

It is not impossible for a person of secure financial means to be a strong Christian, but it has its drawbacks. By trusting ourselves and failing to realize the strength that results from slipping our hand into that of the Almighty, we may find ourselves in a holding pattern just as binding as that of a person who has been stripped of worldly goods. In His providential care, our loving Father may aid us in dropping those weights that hinder our flight.

(9) Sometimes troubles hit in multiples. Normally we can handle one, but two or three or four or five can throw us into an emotional turmoil. **The constant question of "why" can cause us to feel estranged from God.** Perhaps we have not laid the proper foundation for handling problems, or maybe we have made adequate preparation and have even handled some major problems successfully but find ourselves totally unable to cope with a new and unexpected situation. As we scratch and claw for survival, spiritual matters are pushed into the background. In desperation we cry out for God, but He does not seem to be there. We feel all alone.

(10) Problems, crises, emergencies—whatever you want to call them—can either pull us away from God or can draw us nearer, depending upon our attitudes, our backgrounds, and the particular set of circumstances. At other times, however, **our ruts of routine (created by ourselves) can cause us to become comfortable and we forget God.** We may be faithfully attending all the worship services. We may be reading a chapter from the Bible daily. Our normal participation in the various work programs of the church may go on as usual. To the casual observer, we are faithful, diligent Christians. Down deep inside, however, we know that we have lost our closeness to God. We do not depend upon Him because we feel self-sufficient. We are making no significant strides. In the eyes of the world, we

are splendid Christians. But in all honesty, we feel locked in a holding pattern. We are going nowhere.

(11) **Overinvolvement in many worthwhile activities, great pressure, stress, constant demands upon our time, rush, no leisure—in short, burning the candle at both ends—can cause any of us to circle in a holding pattern rather than fly upon our intended course.** It happens to the very best of us. The overinvolvement may be in many noble civic and community projects. It is sad, but true, that a number of Christians are so deeply involved in so many **works of the Church** that real spiritual growth has no time for development. Sometimes we equate **doing** with **being** in Christianity. **Doing** what has been commanded by God and deemed necessary by the local elders is very important in anyone's life. But there must be a proper balance with times of quiet in addition to moments of prayer and study of God's Word. **Being** what we should be is just as important as **doing** what our hands find to do. Sometimes it requires Christian maturity to learn to say "no" to even worthwhile activities when we sense an overcrowding in our spiritual lives. Note the lesson taught in the parable of the soils as it is recorded in Matthew 13:1-23.

Thus, sometimes our own personal problems have so overwhelmed us that we cannot seem to reach out to God and to others. We are no longer flying in a straight course toward our spiritual goals. We are circling repeatedly over the airport, neither landing nor taking off. We are in a holding pattern.

It happens to practically every Christian at one time or another in life.

BIBLICAL EXAMPLE

The story of Elijah as it is revealed in the 18th and 19th chapters of 1 Kings is a familiar one to any Bible student.

Elijah had just experienced a peak in his spiritual life. Standing alone, this prophet had successfully confronted the prophets of Baal on Mount Carmel. After watching the followers of Baal literally cut themselves until the blood gushed out, Elijah calmly took twelve stones and built an altar in the name of the Lord, made a trench around it, placed wood and the animal sacrifice upon that altar, poured four barrels of water on the wood and sacrifice three times, called upon the Lord for fire and watched as the people fell on their faces, proclaiming Jehovah as God. After this momentous event, Elijah's prayer brought rain upon a land suffering from a great drought.

When Jezebel, the queen, was told about Elijah's victorious feats, she threatened him with his life. "So let the gods do to me, and more also, if I make not thy life as the life of one of them by tomorrow about this time" (1 Kings 19:2).

Elijah ran for his life!

After a day's journey into the wilderness, this mighty man of God who had just encountered a most triumphal experience suffered one of the lowest points in his life. Sitting under a juniper tree, Elijah begged God to take his life.

Elijah's physical life was in danger. Jezebel was after his hide. It usually is extremely difficult to maintain the proper kind of spiritual perspective when your very life is in danger.

Concern for physical safety circumvented Elijah's spiritual growth. He needed time to recover—to repair himself. An angel supplied food for his physical body.

Elijah was in a holding position. He wanted to be making progress, but the circumstances of life so weighted him down that he did well to tread water.

There are times when we are like Elijah.

POSSIBLE SOLUTIONS

Just as everyone has a different set of circumstances that sometimes produces a holding pattern, so do the answers differ according to the individual person. The reader will no doubt have personal suggestions to add to those listed below.

(1) **Accept the "rests" in the musical score to be just as important as the "notes" that are played.** Sometimes "just doing nothing" can be quite frustrating. We feel that we aren't doing anything for the Lord unless we are almost frantic with

147

activity. I have experienced the feeling. For months, I did nothing but lie in bed. I couldn't move. I couldn't talk. There were then weeks either in a hospital bed in our den or in a reclining rocker in front of a fire. As I look back over those days now, I realize that they were actually some of the most productive ones in my life. I had been too busy. I needed time to sort things out, to establish priorities. I shudder to think what might have happened if God had not seen fit to provide some rests in the musical score of my life.

(2) **We should all admit that we are only human.** God is certainly aware of the fact. He realizes that human beings will naturally have periods of ups and downs. These patterns are a natural part of life. Sometimes we will circle rather aimlessly, but the circumstances that produced the holding pattern will be resolved and we will once again be back in flight.

(3) **Holding patterns can be hidden avenues for growth.** Just as a seed, we also frequently have to fall apart before we can grow. Sometimes it is good for us to look inward at what is bothering us. Often we are so busy **doing** that we fail to realize what we are **becoming.** Sometimes we need to actively clean the inner house. At other times, we must rest and leave the healing to God. "Create in me a clean heart, O God; and renew a right spirit within me" (Psalm 51:10).

(4) **Recognize the fact that life is filled with circumstances over which we have no control.** Many things will come our way. Some we will bring upon ourselves. Others are completely beyond our realm of influence. They may even "throw us" for a time. Since we **are** only human, there is nothing disgraceful about being discouraged and frustrated. Some time may be required for us to get our bearing. As long as we know our overall goals and trust God that Romans 8:28 is a true promise, we will be able to hold our heads above water until something can be done.

(5) **Holding patterns cause us to realize that we are not as self-sufficient as we once thought.** We can fail. We need God's strength to lean upon. How often our own weaknesses help us realize our true source of power. "For when I am weak, then am I strong" (2 Corinthians 12:10).

"Some doors must be closed before we can see others standing open."

SUGGESTIONS FOR CLASS DISCUSSION

(1) Have you ever experienced the feelings expressed in the first paragraph of this lesson? If you feel like discussing them, share your thoughts with the class.

(2) Give your own definition of a "holding pattern."

(3) How can holding patterns be caused by our sin and stubborn rebellion?

(4) How can holding patterns also be the result of the natural circumstances of life?

(5) If we are truly spiritual, how can something such as the prolonged sickness of a loved one hinder our spiritual growth?

(6) Have there been times when your own physical illness consumed nearly all your thoughts? Did you make any real spiritual growth? What suggestions would you offer to others in the same predicament?

(7) Have you ever had a conflict with a loved one or a close personal friend? How did you handle the situation? How did it make you feel?

(8) Why does the distress of a loved one bother you? Have you ever felt completely frustrated in such circumstances? Were you able to find solutions?

(9) Describe your emotions in the loss of a loved one, whether it was caused by death or some other situation in life. What suggestions would you offer others in the same predicament?

(10) Why is it so emotionally important to feel wanted and to have friends? Is there anything wrong with this feeling? How can moving to a new location intensify this predicament?

(11) Never having known the luxury of material possessions and losing them once you have had them are two entirely situations. Discuss the problems and possible solutions for each type.

(12) Why are we sometimes overwhelmed because of so many problems? Perhaps we had been able to handle all the circumstances up to this point, but the last one is the "straw that broke the camel's back."

(13) What is meant by the term "ruts of routine"? How can they affect our own spirituality? Where does the fault usually lie?

(14) How can spiritual stagnation be produced by an abundance of material possessions? Which do you think can be more trying—a lack or an abundance?

(15) Have you ever been overinvolved in too many **good** things? What were the effects? How did you handle the situation?

(16) Assign one class member the responsibility of relating the incident concerning Elijah. Make the application to our modern Christian lives.

(17) How can the "rests" in a musical score be just as important as the "notes" that are actually played? Have you ever experienced any rests in your own life? What were the end results?

(18) Is there anything wrong with admitting that you are only human? If God understands, why do you think we are so hard on ourselves?

(19) How can holding patterns be hidden avenues for growth?

(20) Cite circumstances over which we have no control.

(21) We all need to realize that we are not self-sufficient. How can there be strength in this realization?

Chapter 13
HOLY MATRIMONY!

*"It is easier to build houses
than to construct homes."*

Just a century ago, divorces were few and far between.
I can remember only one child of divorced parents during my
own elementary school years. In 1975, 1,033,000 divorces
were granted in the United States. The number climbs with
each passing year. Statistics show that 38% of all first marriages fail. Of this number, 79% will remarry and 44% of these
remarriages will fail. In the 1970s, four out of every ten
babies spent at least a part of their childhood in single-parent
homes. That number is also higher today.

All domestic disagreements do not end in divorce, and
there is much discord in the homes that do stay together.
Studies indicate that one-third of all homes have some sort of
domestic violence. Wife-battering has become an epidemic.
(Husband-beating is not even uncommon.)

Although Moses authorized a writing of divorcement
because of the hardness of the people's hearts, "from the
beginning it was not so" (Matthew 19:8). God never intended
for homes to be broken. Marriage was instituted as a lifetime
commitment that could only be broken by the sin of adultery
(Matthew 19:4-9).

Something has gone wrong, even within the Church.
In some way, we Christians must gain a better understanding of marriage and ways to settle inevitable disputes.

DEFINITION OF MARRIAGE

Few couples at the marriage ceremony really have any idea of what marriage is all about or any real understanding of the sacred vows which they make upon that occasion. We, like many other couples, had the promises which Ruth made to Naomi read at our wedding ceremony because they had a special significance to us: "Whither thou goest, I will go." Although we sincerely meant what we promised, there was no way that we could have comprehended the depth of the commitment at that moment.

Simply stated, marriage is a commitment to a lifetime partnership (Mark 10:9). Sexually, socially, emotionally and spiritually, the two become partners in establishing a divine institution—the home. God, in His infinite wisdom, realized that two are better than one when traveling life's journey. It was not good for man to be alone (Genesis 2:18). The promise is made "til death do us part." That's a long time. Much water will flow under the bridge.

True love is not simply a feeling. Feelings come and go in intensity and sometimes fade away. Marriage is a decision— a commitment to a partnership with another person until one dies.

Although Eve was created as a helpmeet for Adam (a helper suitable for the man), the arrangement was also needed for man because it was not good that man should be alone (Genesis 2:18). They truly needed one another. Each complements or completes the other one.

The word "cleave" in Matthew 19 implies being bonded or cemented. The two must break the ties with parents before they can truly be joined or yoked together. Much domestic discord is brought about by the clinging of one or both partners to parents and by failing to be mature enough to stand upon their own feet.

Marriage is a blending of two completely different people. Each brings to the union a different personality, a different background and a different set of values. Neither has the slightest idea of what the future holds. Neither can realistically imagine how well two such totally different personalities can function as one unit. The vows are acts of utter faith with the firm resolution on the part of each to **make** them work.

The promises made at the wedding ceremony are much like a Jewish city. Strong walls were built first to protect the people from the enemy. Then the buildings of the city were erected as the needs developed. Commitment is the wall to the city of marriage.

Marriage is not only a commitment to a partnership designed for the good of each. It is more than a blending of two completely different lives. Marriage is also a union based upon the proper relationship of one party to the other. We call this relationship **subjection**. 1 Peter 3:1 admonishes even the wives of unbelievers to be in subjection. Colossians 3:18 urges wives to submit themselves unto their own husbands. These two passages alone can leave many people with the wrong concept of subjection. It was never intended as a master-slave relationship. The fifth chapter of Ephesians portrays the heart and soul of the husband and wife relationship. The husband is not to be the lord of the submissive wife. Instead, he is to hold her in the same esteem that is used to identify Christ's love for **His** bride, the **Church**. Christ loved the Church enough to die for her! In submission as God intended for it to be, the wife is cherished. She is truly the queen of the home. Her husband adores her. Instead of lording it over her, he shelters her with his love and care. Because of this relationship, the wife is free to develop her beautiful traits to the fullest. Her willingness to entrust her care to her husband causes him to love and esteem her even more highly. It is a delightfully vicious circle!

In considering the definition of marriage, one must view it as a promise of commitment for the four stages of marriage:

(1) from marriage to the birth of the first child;

(2) the period of the births of the other children;

(3) the training of those children as they progress in age; and

(4) the original situation of husband and wife alone.

Each phase has its own set of problems, adjustments and joys. Different problem-solving techniques must be used during the various stages.

The Greeks had four different words for love:

(1) **Eros** meant romantic and sexual—very personal and intimate.

153

(2) **Philia** implied friendly, common interests, goals and companionship.

(3) **Storge** was defined as family love—the love of a mother for her children.

(4) **Agape** was a new word for love, never used before New Testament times. It was a self-giving, sacrificial love—a love governed more by the intellect than the emotions alone (although the emotions were involved). It is this type of love that the husband and wife are to have for one another.

THE THREE ASPECTS OF MARRIAGE

Every human has basic needs that must be met if there is to be happiness and fulfillment. There are physical, emotional and spiritual longings in each of us.

PHYSICAL

(1) Marriage involves a **physical** relationship. It is within the bonds of matrimony that normal sexual drives are to be satisfied. This physical union is honorable and undefiled (Hebrews 13:4). In fact, the seventh chapter of 1 Corinthians very explicitly outlines the sexual obligations of each partner. The Song of Solomon is a delightful commentary on the beauties of physical love.

(2) Sexual fulfillment is only one phase of the physical aspect of marriage. The wife was given the position of the **keeper of the home** (Titus 2:5). It is her responsibility to guide the domestic phase of the home (1 Timothy 5:14). This is not to imply that she must bear the entire responsibility. She may have help from other members of the family (and should), but she is the one in charge. The husband bears the responsibility of earning the living (Genesis 3:17-19) and the wife oversees the management of the home. That is the way that God intended for the responsibilities to be shared in this divine institution. There is certainly nothing within the Scriptures to

indicate that neither can help the other one with the responsibilities, but each has his or her own specific charges. A woman's emotional makeup enables her to act as a thermostat to the temperature of the home. It is she who sets the tone.

(3) Husbands and wives meet the physical needs of the marriage relationship by being **parents** to the children. "A child left to himself bringeth his mother (or father) to shame" (Proverbs 29:15). The father also has major responsibilities in child-rearing (Ephesians 6:4). There is a proper place for both the husband and the wife in the rearing of children. If one or both should neglect responsibilities, then the home cannot function as God intended for it to be.

(4) Another way in which both parties fulfill their obligations to the physical aspect of marriage is by **doing his or her part to help the family live within its income**. It is a very simple rule but so true: any family (whether composed of one or ten members) has to learn to live on its income—no matter what that amount may be. It is a very wise husband and wife who realize this fundamental truth from the beginning and work together in the management of money.

EMOTIONAL

Marriage has its **emotional** obligations as well as its physical ones.

(1) In an ideal marriage, the husband and wife should be on the same wavelength and have the **same basic outlooks and goals in life**. If they saw everything eye to eye, however, the union would be a dull one. The major goals toward which they are striving should be the same ones if there is to be true happiness. Nevertheless, there should be enough variation in personalities to make life spicy. Wouldn't it be terrible to live with someone exactly like yourself!

(2) **Companionship** is one of the most fundamental needs of any human being. Not only should there be

155

a physically sexual attraction between husband and wife, they should also be **best friends**. Friendship and physical love intertwine. How sad it is to feel either deep joy or sorrow and have no one with whom to share the emotion. "Live joyfully with the wife whom thou lovest" (Ecclesiastes 9:9).

(3) **Communicate—communicate—communicate!** Most problems which will inevitably arise in marriage can be handled if only both parties have learned how to express their true feelings to one another from the very beginning. There should be no reason for big problems to develop if husband and wife can sit down with one another and discuss their feelings in a kind, polite manner. It matters not how seemingly insignificant the matter may be. If it is irritating to one party, then it should be discussed for the best solution. Getting it out in the open may enable the offended one to see how trivial the slight may be. Both may be able to laugh over the matter. On the other hand, if the irritation is carefully concealed and buried deeply inside the emotions, it will inevitably fester and cause trouble later on.

Studies have shown that after only two years of marriage, most husbands and wives talk for two or three minutes over breakfast, twenty minutes at dinner and a few minutes in bed at night. By the sixth year, the only time of total communication amounts to ten minutes a day. (The term "communication" goes far beyond idle chitchat concerning the trivialities of the day. It implies a sharing of one's true feelings. Thus, husbands and wives may talk a great deal and yet communicate very little.) Authorities generally agree that a lack of communication is the main problem in 80% of all marriages. Paul Tournier very wisely observed, "Listen to the conversations of our world; for the most part they are dialogues of the deaf."

(4) In marriage, there is **no place for selfishness**. This most intimate of all relationships is based upon a 90-90 rather than a 50-50 situation. There must be a spirit of compromise in which each seeks the good of the other. "Whatsoever ye would that men

156

should do to you, do ye even so to them" (Matthew 7:12). Somehow we manage to apply this golden rule to every relationship except marriage. Both husband and wife should manifest the spirit of Rebekah when she told Abraham's servant that she would draw "water for thy camels also" (Genesis 24:19). It is not love unless the satisfaction of your mate is just as important as your own. Erich Fromm wisely stated, "Infantile love follows the principle: I love because I am loved. Mature love follows the principle: I am loved because I love."

(5) Wise is the mate who realizes that **husband or wife should be placed before the children or parents, other family members, or friends.** Both Genesis 2:24 and Matthew 19:5 teach that we should we willing to leave parents emotionally and physically. This same principle extends to everyone else. Only God should be given preference to one's husband or wife. Just as Ruth was willing to go anywhere with Naomi, so should we place our lifetime partner before all other human beings.

(6) Husbands and wives should **accept one another for what they are**. Marriage is not a reform school. If you don't like the basic personality of your intended, back out of the door—quickly, before any vows are said. Both of you have your own sets of strengths and weaknesses. If your set doesn't blend with that of the one whom you intend to marry, say good-bye before marriage and find another.

Even after a compatible choice has been made and the vows have been spoken, realize that both of you will be constantly changing. After ten years of marriage, neither of you is the same person who made those vows. If you expect him to love you, changes and all, then you must also continually adjust to the different person that he becomes. The negative changes are easier to accept if only we will concentrate on the strengths.

We should learn both to complement and compliment one another. Everyone knows what a "compliment" is. It is simply telling someone something good about themselves. A compliment acts as a stimulus and makes anyone do better. Not as many people are as comfortable with the word "complement." "Complement" simply means "to complete." Most of us are not complete in and of ourselves. We have some good points and quite a few undesirable ones. It is ideal to be united with a person whose strengths supplement your weaknesses. In turn, you do the same for him. Compatibility does not mean that you think exactly the same as your mate but both of you can adapt. Remember that two egos are involved.

(7) A cardinal rule of the emotional side of marriage is **forgiveness**. "Even as Christ forgave you, so also do ye" (Colossians 3:13). Remember that it is only natural that you will hurt one another's feelings from time to time. Both of you will step all over one another's toes. The key is to keep the differences **molehills**. Settle them quickly. Don't let them smoulder. Neither should they be allowed to develop into mountains. When God said, "Let not the sun go down upon your wrath" (Ephesians 4:26), He meant exactly what He said. Irritations that are settled today should never become real problems.

(8) Use **common courtesy**. Isn't it a shame when we treat our pets or even total strangers more politely than we do our mates! 1 Peter 3:8-11 admonished Christians to have compassion and love, be pitiful, be courteous, not rendering evil for evil. (Yes, this applies to husbands and wives as well as to the treatment of every other Christian.) Be fair. Don't impose. Among other characteristics of love mentioned in the 13th chapter of 1 Corinthians is the simple word **kind**. Love is kind. "In her tongue is the law of kindness" (Proverbs 31:26). A world of truth may be found in the words of Proverbs 15:1: "A soft answer turneth away wrath: but grievous words stir up anger." If the words are not already in a couple's vocabulary, they should learn to say **please**, **thank you** and **I'm sorry**. There is no place for nagging in marriage (Proverbs 21:9; 27:15). Luke 6:38 teaches that it is only human nature to respond in like manner: "For with the

158

same measure that ye mete withal it shall be measured to you again."

"To keep love brimming in the marriage cup, when you're wrong admit it. When you're right, shut up" (Ogden Nash).

(9) **Leave some breathing room.** A perfectly good marriage can be strangled. Oneness was never meant to convey this trait. Each person is an independent human being. Instead of an intertwining relationship, the word **parallel** has a better connotation. Both are traveling side by side in the same direction. At first glance, the two lines seem as one (much as a railroad track), but there is some space between the two. Both husband and wife should encourage the hobbies and interests of the other. I do not know the name of the author, but there is a saying that goes, "If you really want something, set it free. If it comes back to you, it's yours forever. If it doesn't, it was never yours in the first place."

(10) **Instilling confidence** is another phase of the emotional side of marriage. The pressures of the world are tremendous on both the husband and the wife. Everyone needs someone to believe in him. (That applies to both male and female.) Anyone loves the person who makes him feel important. Such an ability is far more significant than physical looks. The husband of the worthy woman was known in the gates (Proverbs 31:23). Have you ever wondered what part she played in her husband's status?

(11) **Keep the marriage fresh. Continue the courtship.** It is so easy to take one another for granted and get in a rut. We all tend to neglect our own personal appearances. Put the spark back into a marriage through little thoughtful gestures. Your thoughtfulness would differ from mine because we are married to different people with different needs. Make a list of suggestions for yourself. Always take time to be together by yourselves. It may be leaving the children with someone and taking a weekend vacation. It could be a quiet dinner alone. But you owe it to your mate to

keep a marriage fresh. That just doesn't happen accidentally.

(12) The 13th chapter of 1 Corinthians defines "love": patient, kind, not envious, not egotistical, not selfish, not suspicious, wants to believe the best, wants the mate to do well, believes, hopes, and endures. It's difficult to beat that list!

SPIRITUAL

A marriage that is not built on the right spiritual foundation is indeed on shaky ground from the beginning. An earlier section of this lesson stressed the importance of leaving some breathing room for each party to pursue its own interests. But it was stressed that a common goal—a major thrust in life—is absolutely essential for the success of any marriage. Two people cannot pull in the same direction if each one is following a different map.

There can be a conflict of spiritual goals even when a Christian marries a Christian. One can be very strong in the faith and the other can be lukewarm. There are bound to be disturbances when one wants to attend all the services and devote a great deal of time in teaching and evangelistic opportunities in addition to adequately giving God His portion of the family income. The troubles are compounded when one is a Christian and the other one is not. Such a marriage is Scriptural in God's sight and each must be faithful to the other, but such a union portends deep problems. 1 Peter 3:1 admonishes the wife of an unbelieving husband to teach her mate by translating God's Word into her daily life if he refuses to listen to the actual teaching of the Scriptures. Such a relationship is a strained one to say the least. Every word, every action will be carefully observed by the unbelieving mate.

On the other hand, two strong believers can be more tolerant of one another. Each one realizes that he, too, has moments of weaknesses and can be more understanding of the faults of the other one. When one has difficulties, the stronger one is able to offer encouragement. The blending of two dedicated Christians makes it much easier for each one to live a faithful life.

There are many more opportunities for service open for a faithful Christian couple. They can devote time together in study and growing in the knowledge of God's Word. Visiting in the homes of newcomers, weak members, or in cases of illness is much easier for two than for one. A couple's own home has the potential for becoming a real source of service in the field of Christian hospitality.

In His wisdom, God decreed that one of the requirements for an elder or a deacon is a believing wife. Evidently, Jehovah realized that a man could not adequately serve in such a capacity unless he had a helper at home.

CONCLUSION

The exchanging of wedding rings with the accompanying vows begins a lifetime of togetherness. As the husband and wife mature, so should the marriage.

Home should become a haven, but we must realize that it cannot be a heaven and must not be a hell.

Marriage is divine. It was instituted by God because He must have realized that both parties needed one another physically, emotionally and spiritually.

Our wedding ceremony was recorded on a tape that had previously been used to record the songs at a Sunday afternoon singing service. Several weeks after the ceremony, we listened once again to the vows which we had made. At the conclusion was the song "Sweeter As the Years Go By." It just happened to be at that place on the used tape. We left it there because we thought it was appropriate. Truly, marriage as God intended for it to be becomes sweeter as the years go by.

SUGGESTIONS FOR
CLASS DISCUSSION

(1) Discuss the increase in the number of broken homes and list the reasons (both those presented in the lesson and your own).

(2) Try to briefly summarize a definition of "marriage" that would be pleasing in God's sight.

(3) Is love simply a feeling? What is it? Why is a marriage that is based upon a flippant view of love destined for trouble?

(4) Genesis 2:18 states that it was not good for man to be alone. Why? Do you think that this applies to the woman also?

(5) What is the meaning of the word "cleave" as it is found in Matthew 19?

(6) Marriage is said to be a blending of two completely different personalities. Discuss some typical differences.

(7) The term "subjection" is an integral part of marriage. Why is it for a woman's betterment that she be in subjection to her husband? (Consult the fifth chapter of Ephesians.)

(8) What are the four typical stages of marriage? Add others that you might think are appropriate.

(9) What were the four different words that the Greeks used for our word "love"? Which one applied to married love?

(10) What are the three general aspects of marriage?

(11) Use Hebrews 13:4 and 1 Corinthians 7 in discussing the sexual aspect of marriage.

(12) Why was the wife designated as the "keeper of the home" in Titus 2:5? What does this term imply?

(13) Another physical obligation of marriage is the rearing of children. What parts do both the husband and the wife play in this responsibility?

(14) What part does the management of money play in the obligations of the home?

(15) Which goals in life should be common ones of both husband and wife? What is the value of variations in many of the less important goals?

(16) What are the benefits of husband and wife being best friends?

(17) Communication of actual feelings is one of the most important aspects of marriage. Give some practical suggestions of your own in developing this skill.

(18) Most problems could be avoided if only they were properly handled in the beginning before they become so

enormous. Cite some personal examples of ways in which you have been able to express and resolve minor irritations. Is there anything wrong with differing?

(19) This week, keep a record of the amount of time which you and your spouse spent in actually expressing your feelings to one another. If you would like, share your findings. Were you surprised?

(20) How can selfishness cause trouble in a marriage? What can be done about it?

(21) Do you agree or disagree that the husband or wife should be placed before anyone else? State your reasons.

(22) What does the term "accepting one another" imply? Why is this difficult to do?

(23) What is the difference between "complement" and "compliment"? Why is each essential?

(24) What necessary rule of marriage is implied in Colossians 3:13?

(25) What usually happens to common courtesy after just a few years of marriage? How do you think this situation develops? Is it usually intentional?

(26) What is implied in the admonition to "leave some breathing room" in marriage?

(27) Why does every human being need to be reassured that he is worth something? How can the marriage union be an ideal place for the boosting of one's morale? How can it be devastating?

(28) What are some ways that a marriage can be kept fresh, even after many years have passed?

(29) Why is it so important for a husband and wife to have the same basic spiritual goals? What can happen if they do not?

(30) List ways in which a couple can be of even greater service in the Kingdom if they are working together. Be specific.

(31) Discuss God's wisdom in stating that an elder or deacon must have a wife.

(32) How can a marriage become "sweeter as the years go by"?

Chapter 14
ROOTS AND WINGS

"A baby is God's opinion that life should go on."
—Carl Sandburg

If I had written this chapter when my own children were young, it would have been entirely different. I've learned a lot, but I have found that I still don't have all the answers.

Isn't it strange that just about the time you **get your act together**, it is time for the show to be over!

Sophocles said that children are the anchors that hold a mother to life, but let's be realistic. There are problems in everything, even the blessings of motherhood. The first medication that any new mother should receive is a package of Tums for the indigestion that will be brought about by all the words she'll eat before her child is grown.

What a tremendous responsibility it is to guide a child as he develops in wisdom (intellectually), in stature (physically), in favor with God (spiritually) and man (emotionally and socially)!

EARLIEST INFLUENCES

A child's training actually begins before the baby is even conceived. There is much to be said for the inherited characteristics from earlier generations. They play such an important part in both physical and personality traits.

After birth, there is no stronger influence on the child than the two adults with whom he lives. The characters of both the mother and father will indelibly be stamped upon the baby for life. Any parent would do well to heed the admonition in Judges 7:17: "Look on me and do likewise. As I do, so shall ye do."

It has been said that one of the most important things a father can do for his children is to love their mother. The love of husband and wife should come before the love for the child for this reason: it is essential that the child be able to sense the security of his home. Love for the child naturally follows the love of the parents for one another.

Attitudes are caught, not taught. So much is learned by example. "What you **are** thunders so loudly, I can't hear what you're saying" (Emerson).

ROCKBED FOUNDATION

"To every thing there is a season, a time to every purpose under the heaven . . . A time to get . . . A time to plant . . . A time to keep."

—*Ecclesiastes 3*

Roots and wings are two of the most priceless possessions we can give our children.

The early years are the time for **roots**.

The Scriptures abound in admonitions about the importance of roots. A plant will wither without its roots (Mark 4:6). The Ephesians were to be rooted and grounded in love (Ephesians 3:17). The Colossians were also exhorted to be firmly rooted (Colossians 2:7). A top-heavy tree (full of branches and leaves) without firm roots is destined for trouble. It cannot withstand the storm.

Wringing one's hands over a wayward adolescent will profit nothing. The concern should start at the beginning. Parents have the first quarter of the child's existence in which to prepare him for life on this earth and also for eternity. Too many fail to realize the importance of the menial work of child-rearing. There is a legend concerning some medieval stone masons. When asked what they were doing, one replied, "I am laying bricks." Another answered, "I am building a wall." The third wisely observed, "I am raising a great cathedral." How true!

An Analogy—The life of a child may be compared to a stream of water. A rockbed foundation must be there from the very beginning. There must be a solid layer of **love** in the earliest years. Greater than anything else, this sense of security will mean more than any tangible object that a parent could possibly buy. Loving takes time, but we should find the moments to develop pleasant memories. We **must** take time to talk with our children. Far too many parents yell. Far too few talk. There are literally thousands and thousands of **latch key** children who daily unlock the doors to empty houses. There is no one there with freshly-baked cookies. There is no one to even listen to all the little happenings in the child's day that are so important to him. There is no one to help him sort through the love and the hurts and build some sort of moral foundation for coping with life in general. So many homes are broken ones with only one parent. Far too often, that parent has so little time to really spend with the youngster. In addition to neglect, more than 200,000 American children are abused each year. Statistics show that twelve to fifteen percent of parents abuse their children. In fact, child abuse is the number one killer of children under five years of age from every socioeconomic condition of life.

In addition to love from the parents, a child needs to sense love and acceptance from his own surrounding world. Peer pressure can be terrific, and painful rejection is all too common. A child desperately needs parents to understand what he is facing in his little outside world and help him find solutions.

Love from parents and a child's surrounding world are important. Even more important is another great love—**a love for God**. Even a baby can learn about God. Long before he begins talking, he is absorbing sounds and worldly thoughts that will one day find expression in words. A child should also instinctively be taught about God from the very earliest months. Deuteronomy 6:6-9 outlines the casual manner in which God's Word is automatically taught in every phase of the youth's life. All parents would do well to study these verses.

As a child learns about love (from parents, his surrounding world and God), he should know that he is loved unconditionally for himself. He will make mistakes. We all do. As adults we want to be loved in spite of all our shortcomings. A child needs this assurance even more desperately.

Love develops self-esteem. Everyone has an ego, even a child. It is a healthy thing. If it is damaged early in childhood, the youngster will suffer for life. Everyone will instinctively fight for the preservation of the ego, but it **can** be destroyed. With it goes the emotional death of the individual.

Parents have more to do with a child's sense of worth than anyone else. The child sees himself mirrored in the eyes of his mother and father. Of all people, parents should be sensitive about the child's ego. He has feelings. Don't belittle him. Discipline should enhance the ego, not destroy it.

There is a vast difference between flattery and sincere praise. Children, like pets, can sense when someone truly loves them. It only requires a little searching to find a number of areas in which a child can be sincerely praised.

The wise parent helps the child learn to compensate. **Everyone** has basic weaknesses. A child can be taught that this is natural but he can offset a deficiency by excelling in another field. For example, your offspring may not be athletically inclined; but he may have latent potentialities in musical abilities. The good parent helps the youngster minimize the weaknesses and capitalize on other potentialities. In fact, young people can develop character muscles by learning to overcome weaknesses and various problems in life. If one will only do a little research, he will soon find that most of the outstanding people in the world achieved greatness in their particular field because weakness in another area was the compelling drive to excel in some way.

The developing of a strong sense of self-esteem requires time. We should not be parents unless we are willing to devote the necessary minutes, days and years.

The child should feel, "I am important. I am a child of God. I am loved by God, my parents and those around me. Because I feel sure of myself, I can venture into a challenge. There is nothing wrong with not succeeding in everything."

The waters of life soon begin rushing the child from babyhood into adulthood in only eighteen short years. The rockbed foundation must be there if the child is going to safely guide his raft around the large crags that characterize adolescence.

BANKS OF DISCIPLINE

The banks of the stream are just as important as the rockbed foundation. The banks that keep the child in the right channel are those of **discipline**.

Love is not enough. Proper discipline reinforces correct behavior. Too often we allow the undesirable to be reinforced simply because it is the easiest way out. "A parent who is afraid to put his foot down usually has a child who steps on his toes."

Punishment is something you do **to** the child. It can destroy. Discipline with love is something you do **for** the child. In order for discipline to be effective, it must be consistent, continuous, and done with love and respect. (That advice is easy to give but very difficult to follow!)

The child wants to know what is expected of him. He then feels secure, even with very strict rules. In fact, he feels frustrated if he is not kept within the bounds of what is required. High esteem is developed in homes of security and fair discipline.

Most people think of discipline as punishment for doing wrong. However, the best discipline is reinforcement of the right conduct in the form of praise and acknowledgement. The reinforcement should come soon after the desirable action. **We all tend to repeat whatever is pleasurable.**

There is most certainly a place for **spanking** for most children. The Scriptures very emphatically teach this principle (Proverbs 29:15,17; 22:15; 22:30; 19:18; 13:24). However, there are three general rules that should be followed:

(1) Be reasonable if something occurs accidentally. Any child can spill a glass of milk. Adults do, too!

(2) There should be spanking when there is willful defiance. If the parent says that something must be done and the child willfully refuses, then someone has to give. There is a confrontation. The child must clearly understand who is in charge.

(3) There is an age when other forms of discipline should be used. Spanking is most effective with the young child who has little reasoning ability and no sense of understanding in the loss of privileges.

Most authorities use the age of ten (give or take a couple of years) as the cutoff point for spanking. What is your opinion?

Discipline, or training, teaches a child to stand on his own two feet. Any child who has not been taught to stand alone and function as a worthwhile member of the human race has been deprived, just as much as if he had not received the proper food, clothing, or medicine during the early years. After all, childhood is simply rehearsing for life. Parents only have eighteen years to train this child to be a mature adult and to instill the principles that will affect his eternal destiny.

It is most important early in a child's life to begin giving responsibilities that gradually increase. Some tasks are pleasant. Others are not. Every human being needs to experience the discipline that results from facing the demands of the unpleasant part of life. In assuming responsibilities, the child will make some mistakes. Early in life, he should be allowed to make some decisions and then suffer the consequences. It is essential that he learn to accept the responsibility for his failure. (Note that a child should be allowed to make some decisions and face the consequences, whether they are good or bad. Some decisions should not be left to the child. Which ones?)

THE CRAGS OF ADOLESCENCE

Discipline involves helping the child build a raft to carry him over the crags of the teen years. After a rockbed foundation of love and training, the developing of a child's sense of self-esteem and the building of the banks of discipline, the youth must then face the challenges of the teen years.

These teen years constitute the age of problems. Although they vary with the individual and the circumstances, there is a core than runs through most of them.

(1) Tnere is a normal question of **moral principles**. We teach our children what is right and wrong from God's Word from the earliest years. However, **God has no grandchildren**. Each generation must search the Scriptures for itself and personally accept those principles, not just because Mother and

Daddy have taught that something is right or wrong for years but because the youth has formed his own convictions.

(2) There is an enormous desire for **conformity to peer pressure**. Young people simply do not want to be different from most of their friends. It is just a characteristic of this age. As a parent, I have found two basic principles to be true regarding doing something simply because that is the way everyone else is doing it.

(a) If it really doesn't matter, let the teenager do it. The style may seem ridiculous. If it doesn't violate God's standard of modesty, let him be like the others. Be honest, some of your own teenage fashions seem ridiculous to your children (and even to you now). But you wanted to be like everyone else. Can't you remember?

(b) If conforming to peer pressure and being like everyone else violates a matter of right and wrong in God's sight, then lay the law down and **enforce** it! No parent should allow a child who is still under his authority at home to do anything that is sinful. Naturally, the groundwork for such a stand must be laid during the early years of childhood. It is then that a child learns to respect authority. A parent cannot wait until a youngster is fifteen or sixteen years old before saying "No!"

(3) The **search for identity** is at its strongest point during the adolescent years. Who am I? Where am I going? What do I want to do in life? As parents, we should remember that each child is an individual. They are not carbon copies of ourselves. Neither are they the answer to our own unfulfilled dreams and aspirations. As mentioned earlier, a parent cannot tolerate wrong. In the realm of identity, each child must do his own searching. The wise parent is there as an understanding friend. A teenager's sense of self-esteem (established during the early years) is a determining factor in "finding himself."

(4) **Sexual problems** are intense at this age in life. Early teaching about moral values are put to their

greatest test as the biological urges are the strongest. Countless studies, however, have shown that promiscuity is not the result of overpowering sexual drives. Instead, it results from a low self-esteem. The best insurance for sexual purity is a high degree of personal worth.

How well I remember a graduate class in adolescent psychology at a state university. The professor (and practically everyone else in the class) seemed to think that sexual freedom was only natural and should not be restrained. One day, I asked him what approach he would use if he were working with teenagers and wanted to teach them the importance of sexual purity. In spite of his own lax attitudes, he said: "From the very earliest years I would teach that child that he or she is different with a higher standard than others of that age. A high sense of self-esteem is most important." Although I openly disagreed with his corrupt moral values, I will have to admit that his advice on this phase of the subject has proven to be true.

In this day and age, homosexuality is a sexual problem that must be dealt with. Although there are certain psychological factors that have a bearing on this sexual problem (strong rejection of the parent of the same sex among many others), from the earliest years a child must be taught that homosexuality is sin (Romans 1). It is not simply an "alternate life style."

TIME FOR WINGS

"A time to pluck up that which is planted . . . a time to lose . . . a time to cast away."

—*Ecclesiastes 3*

A child cannot become independent unless he has first been securely **dependent**. (Think about that statement for a few minutes!)

Gradually the grasp is loosened as the apron strings are snipped. God never intended for our offspring to remain at home forever. "Therefore shall a man leave his father and his mother" (Genesis 2:24).

"As arrows are in the hand of a mighty man; so are the children of the youth" (Psalm 127:4). We are simply loaned this new life for a few years. During that time, we must care for his growing body, instill God's principles, teach him a healthy self-respect, and train him in the art of living successfully with other people. (What an awesome responsibility!) Like guests, they stay only a short period of time and then move on as we shoot the loaned arrows from us.

Wise is the parent who voluntarily closes the door to the offspring's new life from the **outside** before interference in adult affairs causes that door to be slammed in his face from the **inside**. It can be done only if parents are mature adults with other interests in their own lives besides their children. The same impulse that prompted them to run after a child when he darted into the street now still urges them to interfere, but they have wisely given him the wings of freedom.

By laying a rockbed foundation and giving the child the roots of love (from parents, from others in the child's world, and from God) and self-esteem (respect of the child for himself), by carefully building the banks of discipline, the parents help a child build a raft strong enough to steer through the crags of adolescence with all its problems. Then the wise parents, with their blessings, give the child wings to become an independent, happy adult with the prospect of a richer life on this earth and a secure eternal destiny.

CONCLUSION

When I feel something very deeply, I search for a piece of paper and a pen. I can best express my feelings in this manner. The first selection below taps my emotions as the "empty nest" syndrome first hit me.

The house is so silent, so deafeningly silent. The hair dryer is still. The shower no longer runs and runs and runs any hour of the day or night. No more of THAT music. No more "Hey, Mom, don't you think you ought to go to the store? I can't find anything to eat."

The rooms are so neat and in order. No more shoes in the middle of the den. No jeans on the floor. No school papers all over the dresser. The closet is so empty and so clean. Nothing clutters the bathroom. It almost looks sterile. The 6'3" "baby" has left home now, and it's just Mama and Papa. When the first one leaves for college you say, "Oh, they'll be in and out. They're still here." Soon you learn better. Slowly you realize and admit that they are no longer at home. They just visit.

As I was walking down the hall, looking at each picture from the earliest baby days to the graduation pictures, I couldn't help but think about all the happenings of those years. The nightly feedings. All the diapers. The toy ducks in the bathtub. The first step. The Bible stories. The years of wrestling with little ones at the worship services. The birthday parties. Costumes for school programs. Homework. Report cards. Camp. Ball games. All the joys and frustrations of growing up.

Where could those years have gone? They were such busy ones that there was no time to even look up, much less realize that time was flying by. Now it's so quiet.

Quite often silence is God's answer to our questions. When Christ prayed in the garden, God's answer was silence. The frustration of silence soon mellows into soul-searching thought, and it is only then that we work our way through to the answers.

My eyes fell on the more formal portraits made during the senior years in high school, and I found my answer. Where had all those years gone?

Just as water goes through several states of matter (solid ice, liquid and then gas), so does time change into different forms. All those years with their many activities are still here. Instead of minutes of the day, they have been changed into the physical, emotional and spiritual makeup of two young adults who each now stand on their own feet as they close one chapter and open the new chapter of adulthood. And parents who are wise will also willingly close one chapter and begin a new one.

After I had watched one of our children leave for a summer's work away from home during the college years, I sat down on the front porch and put my feelings on paper. I would like to use these words as a final bridge to carry the thoughts of one parent into the hearts of other parents.

This is a season of mixed emotions for many women. It is the time of graduations and weddings. The feminine part of the species has been known to shed a few tears at such events—tears mixed with both joy and sorrow: joy over an accomplishment and sorrow because the flipping of the tassel or the walk down the aisle signals the ending of one phase of life and the dawning of a new era. It seems that after those two events, the child is nevermore really at home. If we're realistic about the matter, we'll realize that cutting the apron strings is a God-given instinct. If it were not for that urge, we'd eventually have forty and fifty-year-old children still at home to be cared for.

When you get right down to it, isn't this what we've been working for ever since that little bundle was placed in our arms for the first time? As parents, we became so excited when the baby could hold his head up and then shortly later sit all alone. Most of us entered the exact time of the first step in our baby books because we realized that our child would soon be walking alone. The first words were also noted because we knew that one day soon the child would be able to express his thoughts and wishes to others. Later on we tried to teach him to solve his own problems, learn to manage money and in other ways learn to function independently. We realized that there would be mistakes in judgment; but we were there to support, to encourage him to try again.

As the child grew, we as parents were aware of the fact that we could not make our children carbon copies of ourselves because they have their own abilities and interests. They come through us, but they are not ours to possess. We would be negligent parents if we did not try to instill some of our principles into the hearts of our children—not because they are ours, but because we believe they are founded upon laws set forth by an almighty God who knows what is right.

In Psalm 127, children are compared to arrows—arrows that are sent forth by their parents into the future. At the time of shooting forth the arrow, most mothers and fathers could utter these words to their offspring: "It could not possibly have been eighteen years since you were first placed into our arms. During the time of diapers, middle-of-the-night feedings and days of being tied down with a little child, your leaving seemed so remote. How quickly those years have flown by! As parents, we have made mistakes because we're only human. Please forgive our blunders.

For years we have tried to instill God's principles into your heart because we knew that your eternal destiny is dependent upon following His Word. Now the time has come for you to test those principles, to accept them as your own. You are now an independent adult, and we are so very proud of you. Always remember that although you will be leaving us physically, you can never leave our love and concern because they will go with you to the four corners of the earth. As the arrow is shot forth, we will always be at home watching and praying that the winds of life will not blow you off the course that we have set you upon. Good-bye, my child.

SUGGESTIONS FOR CLASS DISCUSSION

(1) In a brainstorming session, contrast your beliefs concerning child-rearing during earlier years and those you hold to be true now.

(2) When does a child's training actually begin? Cite examples of inherited traits that very strongly affect a person's later years.

(3) The lesson stated that one of the most important things a father can do for his children is to love their mother. Do you agree or disagree? Why?

(4) How are attitudes instilled?

(5) What are two of the most priceless possessions we can give our children?

(6) Read these passages aloud in class and comment on the importance of roots: Mark 4:6; Ephesians 3:17; Colossians 2:7.

(7) Why is it difficult to see the importance of all the menial tasks of rearing children?

(8) A rockbed foundation is essential in a child's life. Why is a solid layer of love so important? Discuss the meaning of love in these areas:
(a) Love of parents;
(b) Love and acceptance from a child's surrounding world; and
(c) Love of God.

(9) More than anything else, what develops a high sense of self-esteem? Why is self-esteem so important?

(10) Discuss the difference between "flattery" and "sincere praise" for the child.

(11) Why does a child need to learn to compensate for his weaknesses during his early years? How can a parent help the child minimize his weaknesses and capitalize on his potentialities? Cite examples from your own experiences.

(12) If one compares a child's life to a stream of water with a rockbed foundation, to what can the banks be likened?

(13) Define "discipline." Is it simply punishment for wrong-doing? Why must good behavior be reinforced?

(14) How can the proper discipline give a child the security that he needs?

(15) Is spanking authorized in the Scriptures? Give examples.

(16) When should a child be spanked? When should he not be punished in this manner? Is there a normal age limit for the effectiveness of such a type of discipline?

(17) Why is childhood the time for the rehearsing of life?

(18) What responsibilities should be given to a very young child? To a child of the elementary school years? To a teenager? Why should he be allowed to suffer the natural consequences for failing to assume his responsibilities?

(19) The teen years constitute the age of problems. Is it normal for a child to question the moral principles which he has been taught? Does God have any grandchildren? Why?

(20) Why is the desire for conformity to peer pressure so great? Discuss the two principles mentioned in this lesson for dealing with this problem. Add others of your own.

(21) What does "the search for identity" mean? Why is it so strong during the teen years?

(22) Sexual problems are intense at this age. What is the best way to deal with them?

(23) How can a parent prevent the sin of homosexuality?

(24) Why is the time for wings just as important as the time for roots? Why is it so difficult for parents to realize that their children are now adults?

(25) Why is it best for parents to voluntarily close the door to their child's adult life from the **outside** before it could be slammed from the **inside**?

Like the bird, who halting in his flight

On limb too light, felt it give way beneath him;

Yet sings, knowing he hath wings.

—Victor Hugo